Retailing, sustainability and neighbourhood regeneration

Michael Carley, Karryn Kirk and Sarah McIntosh

The **Joseph Rowntree Foundation** has supported this project as part of its programme of research and innovative development projects, which it hopes will be of value to policy makers and practitioners. The facts presented and views expressed in this report are, however, those of the authors and not necessarily those of the Foundation.

Published for the Joseph Rowntree Foundation by YPS

ISBN 1 84263 049 0

Cover design by Adkins Design

Prepared and printed by:
York Publishing Services Ltd
64 Hallfield Road
Layerthorpe
York YO31 7ZQ
Tel: 01904 430033; Fax: 01904 430868; E-mail: orders@yps.ymn.co.uk

Contents

Summary

Retail vitality and sustainability in the neighbourhood

Local shopping centres, with their community facilities, libraries, surgeries and pubs are at the social and physical heart of neighbourhoods. This is especially true in regeneration areas, which tend to have a strong sense of community but where many residents are among the almost one-third of British households without a car.

Retail and transport trends have undermined the viability of local shopping in many areas. The advent of large superstores and shopping malls, the consolidation of 70 per cent of retail food spend by large multiple retailers and preference for car-based shopping have meant that more than 60,000 small shops disappear every decade. The trend to car-based shopping contributes to traffic congestion and increased air pollution and CO_2 emissions, which undermine quality of life and Government's commitment to promote sustainable development.

Retail decline is reflected in the dispiriting sight of near-derelict precincts or high streets, with boarded-up shops, which become the focus of anti-social activity. This demoralises communities who value public space. When shops close, poor households have less opportunity to drive to alternative facilities. This can contribute to ill health associated with poor diet. Derelict shopping areas visible to passing traffic contribute to the stigma faced by such neighbourhoods.

Their revitalisation, therefore, is crucial to fostering sustainability, social inclusion and area regeneration. This is a report on retailing in urban regeneration areas, based on 14 case studies around Britain.

Key issues and lessons

The case studies indicate that there is no simple answer to retail regeneration – the solutions which work are as divergent as the retail marketplace and must be tailored to local opportunities. But successful initiatives have some factors in common:

- *attention to the retail marketplace*: clear attention to what is possible within the framework of the local or sub-regional retail marketplace and available catchment area, overlaid with strong aspirations to business success and profitability

- *leadership*: clear leadership in the regeneration initiative

- *involving residents*: respect for local residents' needs and aspirations

- *local vision*: a strong, positive vision for local quality of life, with the retail strategy embedded in the local regeneration or neighbourhood strategy

- *organisational innovation*: control frequently delegated from the local authority to a regeneration company with strong private sector participation or to an experienced community development organisation

- *use of investment*: use of public and social investment to reinforce potential achievement in the marketplace, but not to subsidise marginal schemes

- *environment and community facilities*: promotion of the locality as a high quality destination, and thus footfall, through environmental enhancements and community facilities.

Where projects have been less successful, they have:

- *short-term aspirations*: that dominate development planning

- *lack of vision and strategy*: pursuing of partnership without achieving a clear vision and consensus on future aspirations, and thus a clear, agreed strategy

- *failure to work towards sustainability*: ignoring the need to achieve economic, social and environmental objectives simultaneously, which defines the term 'sustainable' development.

Many more specific issues are discussed. Among these are the following.

Restore or demolish and rebuild?

An important question is whether to restore existing facilities, often the only choice in a high street in multiple ownership, or to demolish and rebuild, which is especially important for 1960s'-style shopping precincts. Advantages and disadvantages to both are discussed.

Phasing of regeneration and housing policy affect retailing

The phasing of regeneration, especially demolition of housing in the shopping catchment area and the decanting of population elsewhere, can have a major impact on the commercial viability of existing retail facilities, especially those operating at the margins of profitability. Housing policies and regeneration

programmes, which tend to concentrate the lowest income households in ever fewer estates, also have a negative impact on retail vitality on these estates. Too often, in the case studies, the demolition of a shopping precinct or market has meant the loss of local retailers who go out of business, retire or relocate elsewhere in the city. But some initiatives have fostered local retail vitality through business support and advice, or by making transitional arrangements during regeneration.

The role of community, health and social facilities, and public space, in creating vibrant shopping centres

The best neighbourhood and district centres, lively and with ample footfall, combine retail provision with a range of community and health facilities, including libraries, healthy living centres, employment centres, education and training facilities, and so on. The social focus is a complement to the retail focus, and both reinforce the sense of destination and 'place' which underpins retail vitality and serves community needs.

Meeting market needs for retail space

Successful initiatives provide shop units of appropriate sizes to both market and retailer needs, ranging from market stalls, to small kiosks, to giant superstores. All can have a role to play. Small units, such as kiosks, can serve as low-risk 'stepping-stones' into the retail marketplace for budding local entrepreneurs, especially if marketing advice and business support are available.

Extension of catchment area beyond the locality

There are real economic and social advantages in increasing the catchment area. One approach is to physically reorganise facilities, so that they are visible, attractive and appear a secure, pleasant destination to passing non-residents. Another is to develop a shopping centre marketing strategy, which builds on a particular market niche. Successful marketing strategies are cited, which can represent joint effort of retailers and the local authority.

Vulnerable position of traditional market halls

If these are within covered structures, they may be unsound and require major investment that is not available. One option is to let the market run down to the point of closure; another, if the land is valuable, is to close the market and sell on the land, thus realising a capital receipt.

Either way, the market does not survive. Given the historic role of such markets in British retailing, there is case for 'listing' to preserve their function.

Local employment benefits

Although there is little sound evidence of whether new retail development creates new employment, or merely displaces it, a significant finding is that in some cases where retailers set out specifically to provide employment opportunities for long-term unemployed local residents, they were successful in doing so. This suggests that training and employment schemes, with strong retailer commitment, have real potential to contribute to reduction of unemployment, particularly as the 'sequential' land-use test makes inner city and brownfield sites more attractive to large retailers.

Improving environmental benefits and fostering good urban design

The best refurbished and new developments not only improve retail vitality but also contribute to quality of life in the neighbourhood by environmental improvements, historic building restoration, creation of quality public space, use of public art and development of community facilities such as healthy living centres. However, too many developments still achieve retail vitality at the expense of quality urban design. This is particularly the case with shopping centres dominated by car parks, which turn their back on the neighbourhood for security reasons. The report calls for urban design guidance to improve the quality and sustainability of development.

Failure to embrace broader needs for sustainability

The contribution of CO_2 emissions from traffic to climate change is now accepted. Unfortunately, many of the initiatives explored in the case studies achieved retail vitality by attracting yet more car-borne shoppers, with increased flows of traffic seen as a mark of success. This is not an issue resolved only at the local level. The report argues that, if national objectives of reducing CO_2 and other emissions are to be met, at a time when traffic volumes are still increasing, national targets need to be translated into regional and local targets, and that every development should include an assessment of CO_2 implications and promote sustainable transport modes: walking, cycling and public transport.

The case studies

Case studies were selected to represent a range of development challenges, including refurbishment of existing local shopping precincts, parades of shops, high streets and market halls (Chapter 4); and demolition and rebuild of shopping centres and even construction of new high streets and market halls (Chapter 5). A final case study looks at a large shopping mall on brownfield land. The case studies were also selected because each initiative has made significant achievements in retail regeneration. As such, the 14 case studies provide a wealth of information on good practice. Each case study identifies 'points of inspiration' or best practice but also 'constraints on regeneration', which are areas of lack of achievement or unresolved issues.

Conclusions and recommendations

The report concludes that more strategic approach to retail revitalisation would extend and further enable the retail achievements and good practice documented in the case studies, and help local stakeholders overcome constraints.

Recommendations include the following.

- *National planning guidance*: planning guidance should be enhanced to foster strategic retail planning at the regional and development plan spatial levels, and set out the factors of analysis which enable retail trends, transport and land use planning options and the need to balance town centre, and district and neighbourhood, function at a time of contracting opportunity for smaller,

independent retailers. An appropriate balance of retail function in prosperous and deprived areas should receive attention, by making the sequential test yet more sophisticated. PPG 6 should give greater emphasis to the social impact of the location of new retail development, particularly superstores and supermarkets.

- *Regional planning guidance* (for England, and its equivalent for Wales and Scotland) should integrate need for retail vitality and area regeneration within a broader context of sustainable development including integration of transport and land use. The need to reduce CO_2 emissions by planning should also feature strongly in guidance. The need to consider parking charges at most retail locations, in and out of town, should be considered, including the opportunity to hypothecate parking revenues to sustainable transport modes.

- *Local authority development plans*: the 'hierarchical' framework for retailing which enables sequential testing should be further developed to encompass support for regeneration, and the role of district and neighbourhood centres in social and economic life. Local authorities' development plans should encompass retail analysis and 20-year forward strategies for retail location and enhancement.

- *Neighbourhood/district retail strategies*: the decline of local retail viability and vitality should be managed and countered within the context of both top-down development planning and local, bottom-up retail development strategies, which encompass residents' social and environmental aspirations. Forums as proposed by PAT 13 would take forward this activity, but they need to concentrate on articulated strategy or they will be seen as 'talking shops'.

- *Local authority liaison officer on retail enhancement*: every local authority concerned about the quality of retailing in and out of regeneration areas would benefit from designating an officer to develop intelligence and competence in this area. The officer would be available to assist local retail development partnerships with retail assessment and strategy, to monitor retail viability and vitality, and to promote the case for retail area enhancement within planning and economic development processes.

- *Retail development within context of Community Planning framework*: partnership 'fatigue' suggests a simplification of organisational arrangements and a straightforward means for stakeholders to interact with the local council. The emerging Community Planning framework, at the neighbourhood or area level, provides a good context for achieving local involvement in retail revitalisation.

1 Local shopping, climate change and social inclusion – not so strange bedfellows

Despite phenomenal growth in numbers of hypermarkets and out-of-town centres over the past ten years, retail and transport trends have contributed to a decline in shopping opportunity for the almost one-third of Britons living in households without cars, or who are too infirm to drive, many of whom are in disadvantaged neighbourhoods. This reinforces social exclusion and ill health associated with poor diet. It also supports a continuing shift to car-based shopping which has major environmental impacts, such as increasing the transport contribution to CO_2 emissions – at a time when control of the greenhouse gases which contribute to climate change is a pressing challenge.

Car-based shopping also contributes to the decline of shopping areas in local neighbourhoods as households with cars travel further afield, often to shopping centres with parking for 6,000 cars or more. Some declining shopping environments are in regeneration areas where large amounts of public funds are attempting to reverse decline, but lack of 'joined-up' policy and weak strategic planning mean there has been little co-ordination over the location of large retail facilities between local authorities, themselves sometimes in intense competition for inward retail investment.

Much of the policy focus in retailing has been on city centre vitality, clearly an important issue. But receiving less attention are the thousands of district and local retail centres outside of prime city centres and designated regeneration areas, many of which are in decline. At a time when major environmental and personal health benefits could be gained from shifting millions of short car journeys to walking, cycling and public transport, and when social benefits could be gained from strong neighbourhood centres, allowing local retailing to decline undermines the potential of the sustainable development of Britain's neighbourhoods.

Retail decline is reflected in the dispiriting sight of high streets with boarded-up shops, or near derelict precincts on estates. This makes life difficult for households on low incomes, as they are reliant on local supermarkets and corner stores rather than on superstores or out-of-town supermarkets (Robinson *et al.*, 2000). Retail decline demoralises communities who value public space; shopping areas are the focus of community life and the location of libraries, surgeries, pubs and community organisations. The dereliction of shopping areas visible to passing traffic contributes to the stigma faced by declining neighbourhoods.

Shops at the heart of neighbourhoods ... neighbourhoods at the heart of sustainable development

Locally, whatever their condition, shopping centres are commonly viewed by residents as at the physical and social heart of their neighbourhood. Nationally, efforts to achieve sustainable development and social inclusion are now putting neighbourhoods at the heart of policy implementation, for example, through the National Strategy for Neighbourhood Renewal and the Community Action Plans required by the Local Government Act 2000. This local focus for achieving national policy objectives is reflected in the Prime Minister's recent attention to local 'liveability' as a key to quality of life. It is an appropriate perspective because sustainable development at the neighbourhood level has been described as the foundation of national sustainability – in 'a chain' of local, citywide, regional and national efforts only as strong as its weakest link (Carley, 1999). And it has long been recognised that social inclusion is only achieved by linking bottom-up and top-down effort.

A general challenge to sustainable development is that rhetoric is yet to be matched by sufficient achievement on the ground, even though Local Agenda 21 (LA 21) has now been with us for almost a decade. However, its record has been described as 'marginal, institutionally and in terms of effects' (Cameron, 2000). Given that the Local Government Act puts sustainability explicitly at the centre of local policy and implementation, an important task therefore is to seek out innovative solutions which are being 'tested' in practical developments in local neighbourhoods. In terms of neighbourhood retailing, this is a focus of this study.

Although the condition of many local retail centres is pressing, it is within regeneration areas that the worst problems, but also innovative solutions, can be found. This is because of committed public investment, formal attention to regeneration strategy and the many partnerships already operating in every regeneration area. These partnership arrangements are instructive because the use of

partnerships as a means of governance is spreading – into planning for the whole local authority, into the Community Planning initiative and the recent requirement for Local Strategic Partnerships, and into retail enhancement, with the Business Improvement Districts recently proposed by the Prime Minister. The link between partnership and retail strategy needs to be understood, for partnership and strategy are two sides of the coin of local regeneration (Carley *et al.*, 2000a).

This, then, is a report on retail revitalisation in urban regeneration areas, based on 14 case studies around Britain. The research takes an integrated perspective across three policy sectors: retail vitality and viability;[1] social inclusion and area regeneration; and sustainable development. The latter is particularly with regard to the relationship between transport, air pollution and climate change, but also with concern for the local environmental and urban design impact of retail developments.

A number of local retail revitalisation projects are addressing at least some of these issues. There are some real success stories in increasing the availability of shopping provision for local residents, in extending catchment areas to foster retail vitality, and in providing regenerated physical and social community centres which are a hub for regeneration and which link new shops to refurbished social facilities such as libraries, health centres, community cafés and offices for community organisations. These successes, but also limitations in regeneration achievements, particularly in failure to integrate or achieve environmental benefits from retail regeneration, are reported in the case studies in this report.

Aims of the project

The aim of this project is to further understanding of the potential for retail revitalisation schemes to contribute to social inclusion and local sustainability development by:

- studying a range of attempts at retail regeneration in disadvantaged neighbourhoods in the form of community shops, precinct and high street renewal, and new shopping centre and high street developments, documenting the successful and less successful characteristics of projects from social, environmental and economic perspectives

- understanding the conditions under which retailers will invest in regeneration areas

- assessing potential directions for local action, such as local retail strategy development, which, combined with changes in national policies, including planning policy, could achieve simultaneous benefits in regeneration and sustainable development.

Neighbourhoods and retailing: to the fore in the policy agenda?

A number of policy threads are coming together which may potentially influence retailing in local neighbourhoods. At best, these offer a real chance to establish a participative framework of local action and empowerment which could, over some decades, foster healthier local neighbourhood centres, and thus the sustainable development of neighbourhoods and cities

themselves. At a more general level, this could contribute to enhanced local democracy and social inclusion.

At the core of this policy agenda are the now explicit responsibilities of local authorities in England to promote the social, environmental and economic well-being of communities, and to develop community strategies in partnership with local residents (DETR, 2000). Hopefully, these will not be as weak as most LA21 plans. Community strategies should include local retail strategies based on a retail audit. The condition of local shops may be a good starting point for the development of community strategies, because it is an issue of concern to many people from all walks of life. Options for retail strategies based on practical developments are described in the case studies of this report, with a suggested audit framework given in Appendix 1. At the local level, community strategies may be supported by Local Public Service Agreements, which set out aims and responsibilities for public service provision.

Local retailing in some areas will also be supported by the proposed Business Improvement Districts (BIDs), announced by the Prime Minister in April 2001. BID zones will be designated and in those areas, if a majority of companies agree, a company will be formed under joint ownership of local businesses and the local authority. The establishment of BIDs will require legislation and they may be a few years off. It remains to be seen if they will be designated outside of city centres, or if they will have legal authority to raise capital loans for substantive development projects.

Although, as the case studies will demonstrate, much innovation can be put in train locally, support at the city-wide, regional and central government levels is also important. At the strategic or local authority-wide level, the formation of Local Strategic Partnerships (LSPs) can serve not only to bring residents and retailers into the strategy process, but also to support neighbourhood plans with broader policy. For example, if public investment is to be targeted to shopping in regeneration areas, then other initiatives, such as Unitary Development Plans, may need to support regeneration overtly. Local retail strategies linked to local plans could be a vital component of the regeneration framework. These local planning frameworks would then need to be supported by planning policy guidance and by appeal decisions taken by the Secretary of State.

At the regional level, development plans by Regional Development Agencies, and regional planning guidance prepared by Government Offices, ought to support not only retail vitality but also sustainable development in all forms. It remains to be seen if they will do so, and if these efforts will be integrated to form a coherent regional framework. Currently, there is no statutory requirement for local plans to conform with regional planning guidance, or for issues of sustainable development to be integrated with economic development strategies. At a national level, neighbourhood interests will be represented by the Neighbourhood Renewal Unit at the Department of Transport, Local Government and the Regions (DTLR), which is intended to disseminate good practice from place to place.

Finally, it is important to note that, as more partnerships in LSPs and BIDs are proposed, there is concern over 'partnership fatigue' associated with too many local partnerships sapping available human resources. Partnership

rationalisation is therefore important, both at local authority and neighbourhood level. There is evidence that local people prefer one overall partnership which deals with most aspects of quality of life and which provides a single gate to institutional stakeholders, particularly the local authority. Decentralisation initiatives in many local authorities, linked to Best Value provision and service quality, can play an important role in streamlining local participation so that it is effective and does not contribute to partnership fatigue. If decentralisation is genuinely empowering, public investment will have a community-led focus that ought to cause more joined-up policy and practice. It could also encourage public sector interventions, whether in planning or regeneration, that systematically influence the direction of market-led retailing to engender not only retail vitality but also sustainable development and social inclusion.

Methods of the study

The project began with desk research of relevant literature, documented in the references, followed by selection of case studies in designated regeneration areas – following advice from a telephone survey of expert informants. The criteria for case study selection was to pick initiatives which, although not perfect, had made significant progress in achieving retail regeneration, and would therefore allow learning to be unlocked about that process and constraints on it. A set of criteria for examination of the case studies was developed, reflecting the project's three-fold concern for retail, social and environmental issues. A summary of the criteria is presented in Table 1.

The project's fieldwork consisted of: two to three site visits to the 14 case study areas; an average of 12 one- to two-hour face-to-face interviews with participants in each of the case studies, including regeneration managers, local government officers, shopkeepers and retail managers, community representatives and other stakeholders; a small number of focus groups with local residents/shopkeepers and local government officials. Finally, there were face-to-face interviews with development policy managers from major food chains, retail specialist chartered surveyors, retail investment companies and retailers' organisations such as the National Retail Planning Forum.

Table 1 Main criteria for assessment of case studies

Issues	Criteria
Retail	• Has the development process restored retail *viability and vitality* to the area?
	• Has the *range of shops and/or product lines* available increased?
	• Have *existing retailers/stallholders* been protected during the regeneration process?
	• Is the intended *catchment area* appropriate to the scale of retail provision?
	• Does the development assist *local entrepreneurship* in the retail sector through business support and/or premises?
	• What *innovation* is demonstrated in fostering retail regeneration?
Social	• Have local residents, particularly the unemployed, gained *training and employment benefits* from the development?
	• Has retail development been linked to the development of premises for *social, health and voluntary organisations* to create a lively, multi-use destination?
	• Has the development strengthened local *community organisation(s)*?
	• Has the development process contributed to the *asset base of the community*?
	• How have issues of *crime and anti-social behaviour* been addressed?
Environmental	• Has there been an effort to foster use of *sustainable transport modes*: walking, cycling, public transport?
	• Has there been attention to the need to *reduce vehicle emissions*, such as CO_2?
	• Does the development demonstrate *high quality urban design*, and make a positive, sustainable (long-lasting) contribution to the area?
	• Does the development indicate concern for *recycling*, including of premises and building materials?
	• Is the *environment* of the centre managed in an effective manner?
Partnership	• Have local residents had the opportunity to be *active participants* in the regeneration process?
	• Has the full range of *appropriate stakeholders* been included?
	• Are there particular points of innovation in the *contribution of the private sector* to regeneration?

Case studies

The case studies have been selected to give a range of types of local regeneration initiatives, including refurbishment and new build of shopping centres and even high streets, and also initiatives aiming for differing spatial scales in catchment areas: local, sub-regional and regional. They also range across inner city, peripheral estate and a former industrial town in the Rhondda Valley. Case studies were also selected because each has an element of innovation and success, which could inspire and/or be replicated elsewhere. Not surprisingly, each case study had limitations as well, and these have been documented and will also inform discussion of issues in the next chapter. The chapter numbers referenced in Tables 2, 3 and 4 are for this report.

Table 2 List of case studies: 'Refurbishing existing local shopping centres and high streets' (Chapter 4)

Location	Description
Existing shopping precincts	
Muirhouse, Edinburgh	Refurbishment of a precinct of retail and social facilities in one of Edinburgh's most disadvantaged areas. The former centre includes a new community library and arts centre with garden.
Castlemilk, Glasgow	Estate centre refurbishment anchored by a food retailer in one of Scotland's four flagship regeneration areas. Includes new 'kiosk shops' to encourage local retail initiative.
Castle Vale, Birmingham	Housing Action Trust initiative including rebuilding of a shopping centre by J. Sainsbury, providing 400 new jobs. Includes nursing home, community restaurant, arts programme and an anti-crime strategy.
Existing parades of shops	
Longley Estate, Sheffield	A resident association initiative to renovate local shops, create employment and capture local spending, including community-owned shop, café, welfare advice and health project.
Bradbury Street, Hackney	Shopping street regeneration, café, managed workspaces and innovative kiosk initiative by non-profit organisation to encourage start-up and sustainability of local retail businesses.
Existing high streets	
Upperthorpe, Sheffield	In an inner city area, regeneration of local shopping centre including healthy living centre and library.
Ferndale, Rhondda	In former coalmining town, a major community centre/cinema in a significant church, renovated by a community development trust.
Green Street, Newham	Including both high street and market, in an ethnically diverse neighbourhood, growing from a local centre to a specialist Asian shopping destination with a regional catchment area.

Table 2 List of case studies: 'Refurbishing existing local shopping centres and high streets' (Chapter 4) (cont'd)

Location	Description
Existing market hall Borough Market, Southwark	Revitalisation of a market established in 1756 by a Development Trust administered by trustees who live or work in the local neighbourhood.

Table 3 List of case studies: 'New shopping areas within integrated regeneration initiatives' (Chapter 5)

Location	Description
New high street Crown Street, Glasgow	Regeneration initiative in the Gorbals to create a new but traditional urban neighbourhood including owner-occupied homes, social housing and new shops.
New shopping centres Pennywell, Sunderland	In Sunderland's most deprived area, complete rebuilding of the estate's 15-unit shopping centre linked to new neighbourhood family support centre.
Seacroft, Leeds	Rebuilding of a district shopping centre. Includes Tesco New Deal initiative to invest in inner city locations and to link retailing to employment creation.
New shopping centre plus new high street Hulme, Manchester	Retail regeneration including a new superstore supporting new market hall and high street.

Table 4 List of case studies: 'Regional shopping centre' (Chapter 6)

Location	Description
Braehead, Renfewshire	A major regional centre on a brownfield site, including consideration of the impact on nearby Social Inclusion Partnership areas.

Outline of the report

The next chapter describes key environmental and social trends that provide the context for retail revitalisation in local neighbourhoods. Chapter 3 draws on the case studies to discuss the key generic issues and lessons of retail revival in urban regeneration areas. Chapters 4, 5 and 6 discuss the case studies, giving for each a synopsis and listing 'points of inspiration' where things have worked well, as well as 'constraints on regeneration', which are limitations of the retail regeneration process. A concluding chapter documents recommendations to arise from the analysis.

2 Environmental and social trends influence local shopping

Shopping, social inclusion and climate change: joined-up governance is essential to multi-faceted challenges of sustainable development that are characterised by dynamic interaction between economic, social and environmental factors. This three-way relationship is at the heart of most definitions of sustainable development (Carley and Christie, 2000). Understanding global and local trends that influence retailing is vital to fashioning appropriate solutions. This chapter examines those trends.

Climate and cars

Evidence for the planet's changing climate, sometimes called global warming, is nearly incontrovertible, thanks to continuing scientific analysis by the UN's Intergovernmental Panel on Climate Change (Houghton, 1997). New evidence for this disturbing phenomenon emerges daily, from shrinking glaciers to changes in the seasons. A main cause is greenhouse gases, so called because they reflect the sun's heat back onto the planet, instead of allowing it to radiate into space. This 're-radiation' warms the atmosphere.

A major culprit is the gas CO_2, of which more than a quarter of emissions come from motor vehicles. The Government is committed to reducing CO_2 levels by 20 per cent on 1990 levels by 2010.[1] On current trends, just to stabilise these emissions at present levels requires drastic action to cut back what has been called 'automobility' (Carley, 1992). The prospects are not good: vehicle ownership and use are rising, in a country that has one of the highest rates of vehicle take-up of road space in

the world (Carley and Spapins, 1998). Further traffic growth of 32 per cent by 2010 is predicted; with a possible 69 per cent increase in vehicle numbers in the UK by 2025 (*The Times*, 26 March 2001, p. 13). The Government's best hope is that it can reduce the rate of growth but not alter its upward trend.

Driving to the shops

Many of these car journeys in Britain are to retail premises: superstores, shopping malls, outlet 'tin sheds' along the motorway and so on. Parking provision for 6,500 cars at a mall is not untypical, with a single mall generating nine million vehicle trips per year. Even a modest superstore will generate 1.5 million vehicle movements per year.

Changes in retailing have brought economic benefits and social impacts, including on traffic. There has been a polarisation of retail activity away from neighbourhood shopping streets and parades into city centre and out-of-town, purpose-built locations. In the latter, 95 per cent of shoppers arrive by car (Carley, 1996). From a very low base in 1980, out-of-town shopping will account for a third of all retail sales in the UK by 2005 (verdict cited in *The Independent*, 24 March 2001). Such out-of-town sales increased by 6.4 per cent in the year 2000 alone and are expected to grow by 34 per cent over the next five years.

Car-borne shopping has become a way of life. This contributes to the decline of neighbourhood and district centres, reinforced by other trends. For example, shopping areas that have a catchment with a declining population, typical of regeneration areas, find it even more difficult to remain viable.

This report explores case studies in such areas which have suffered economic, social and demographic decline, but which have managed, against the odds, to increase the catchment for local shops. But it is not entirely 'win–win' from a sustainability point of view. In areas desperate for inward retail investment, more traffic equals more customers. This is too often seen as a good thing.

Car-borne shopping is not a way of life for households without cars: poor, inner city residents; residents of peripheral estates; and those from former industrial villages miles from the shops and connected by infrequent public transport. Return bus fares to the supermarket of £5 are not uncommon. Where no public transport exists, or a mother is burdened with a pram and shopping, an expensive taxi may be the only option.

At a national level, as Table 5 shows, of the poorest 30 per cent of all households, more than half have no car and, in the poorest decile, only

Table 5 Non-car-owning households by decile of gross income

Decile	% households with no vehicle ownership
Lowest income decile	81.8
Second	72.9
Third	51.5
Fourth	34.4
Fifth	23.7
Sixth	14.1
Seventh	10.6
Eighth	6.3
Ninth	4.3
Highest income decile	2.5

Source: Family Expenditure Survey, 1995–96.

18 per cent of households have a car. Overall, there are around 6.9 million households in Britain without a car, around 30 per cent of the total number.

Trends in retailing

In part, car-borne shopping has been encouraged by consolidation in the retail sector into fewer, larger shops – multiple food retailers as a whole having more than 70 per cent of the market. There is further consolidation on the cards, with the introduction by big chains of both smaller- and larger-format stores, but also by buying out small competitors, such as nearby chemists, and then replicating them in-store.

One outcome is that independent retailers suffer a relentless decline with 60,000 shops closing every ten years. For example, the numbers of independent grocers fell from 116,000 in 1961 to only 20,900 in 1997 (Select Committee on Environment, Transport and Regional Affairs, 1999). A similar change has taken place in the comparison sector where a large proportion of outlets are owned by a small number of companies. The economies of scale offered by these large companies have made them more competitive. These facts are salient for area regeneration practitioners, who must work with the marketplace to promote social inclusion.

As small retailers close, more people have to, or want to, drive to large stores to meet their daily needs. For some, this represents a freedom of choice in shops, product range and prices, which is seen as a boon of modern life. This type of shopping has been encouraged by the fact of more women working, with less time to shop, growing rates of car ownership, increased ownership of freezers and microwave ovens.

Modern retailing is a two-edged sword – we may decry the trends, such as traffic growth or the spread of shopping malls, but many of us enjoy the benefits, including a decline in the real price of food of 9.4 per cent from 1989 to 1998 (Monopolies Commission, 2000).

Nor are the trends all one-way. Retail location policy has shifted since the early 1990s (Carley, 1996). There are now attempts to rein in out-of-town shopping, which has given rise to policy guidance on retailing (PPG 6) and transport (PPG 13), which emphasise in-town shopping over out-of-town locations in a 'sequential test' (see also Ecotec Research and Consulting and Transportation Planning Consultants, 1993; House of Commons Environment Committee, 1994).[2] But most policy research has been concerned with out-of-town shopping vis-à-vis city centre vitality, rather than with neighbourhood shopping or area regeneration (see, for example, Chase *et al.*, 1997; Hillier Parker, 1997; *The Independent*, 1998a, 1998b; URBED, 1994).

Planning permissions 'in the pipeline' mean that the policy impact has been weak with shed-type hypermarkets and 'factory outlets' opening frequently. A single company, Freeport Leisure, opened three-quarters-of-a-million square feet of out-of-town space in 1999 (Colliers Erdman Lewis, 1999). In September 1999, Boots, long a champion of in-town locations, announced that it was bowing to market pressure and opening 160 new out-of-town stores (*The Independent*, 1999a).

Retail policy has become the focus of intense interest with the purchase of Asda by the American out-of-town giant Wal-Mart, whose market capitalisation is ten times that of its nearest UK competitor, with turnover of $130 billion per year. Wal-Mart's global buying power brings lower prices, identified by the Prime Minister as of potential benefit to low-income households, but at the price of the erosion of retail function in surrounding areas (*The Independent*, 1999b). American research suggests that Wal-Mart's expansion in the decade 1986–95 resulted in the closure of 7,326 shops in the United States (*The Observer*, 1999). But investment by large supermarkets can also be a driver of regeneration, as reported in a number of case studies here.

The employment impact of new developments is also a matter of concern, with out-of-town proponents arguing that new jobs are created, and in-town supporters suggesting that jobs are merely transferred or that the number declines as smaller shops go under (see, for example, Boots the Chemists, 1998; EDAW for Tesco, 1999; London Economics, 1995; National Retail Planning Forum Research Group, 1997; Townsend *et al.*, 1996). This is important as retailers frequently cite the job creation benefits of new developments, but with little or no analysis available of the number of jobs lost in shops and market stalls closed. Some case studies in this report suggest employment benefits for local, unemployed residents are possible from retail investment, if the process is effectively managed.

Shopping and social exclusion

There are many people who have less chance to enjoy the benefits of modern retailing and yet who frequently suffer the costs. These include the 30 per cent of less well-off households without access to a car, and vulnerable people such as elderly persons and child pedestrians. The closure of small shops and other trends in transport, such as buses caught in traffic jams, contribute to the social exclusion suffered by people who have to make do with poor shopping and high prices.

The restructuring of retail activity over the past two decades has not taken into account the impact of this process on disadvantaged neighbourhoods. It has been market-led, with mobile consumers with high spending power having had the greatest influence over location decisions. Improved retail facilities, particularly supermarkets, have drawn the affluent shoppers away from disadvantaged neighbourhoods, threatening viability of the remaining stores and reducing the service for the residents unable to travel. The lack of local shoppers discourages investment, contributing to decline, which may add to the disparity in health between rich and poor. For example, Acheson's inquiry into poverty and ill-health found that a characteristic which distinguished deprived from prosperous neighbourhoods was a dearth of shops supplying quality food at reasonable prices (Acheson, 1998). Access to nourishing, affordable food is an obvious prerequisite for sustainability.

Some retailers are said to exploit their monopoly position in neighbourhoods where income and car ownership are low. However, the British Retail Consortium argues that retailers are:

... caught up in the same circle of decline in socially vulnerable areas together with schools, doctors' surgeries and other important amenities. It is a chicken and egg argument whether decline is accelerated by the demise of shops or whether shops close and leave because it becomes increasingly difficult to make a living.
(Ann Robinson, quoted in *The Independent*, 3 February 1999)

Deprived areas have not been a target for retail investment because of the lack of available spending power of the residents and the stigma of the areas limiting the catchment population. However, an exception has been discount supermarkets, which see these areas as a niche market – particularly if they can achieve low set-up costs. A recent development is that restrictions on the availability of suitable development sites because of tightening of planning control are directing large retailers to regeneration areas. Seacroft Green in Leeds is a case in point.

While improved retail facilities, especially supermarkets, offer considerable benefits to residents in disadvantaged urban neighbourhoods, many of the advantages are based on the ability to buy in bulk. Small households and people on restricted incomes may not be able to afford these offers especially if they have poor food storage facilities.

Summary of trends in retailing and transport

Trends in retailing and transport which can contribute to the social exclusion include the following (Carley, 1996):

- *Shift to larger retail outlets and closure of smaller shops*: between 1990 and 1995, the number of independent bakers fell by 32 per cent, grocers by 22 per cent and butchers by 10 per cent. Local traders need only 10 per cent erosion of custom to trade at a loss.

- *Shift to out-of-town shopping*: with 70–90 per cent of out-of-town trade 'cannibalised' from existing retail centres,

11

and around 95 per cent of out-of-town shoppers arriving by car.

- *Consolidation of market share*: major retailers have wholesale buying power not available to independents, making local shops expensive by comparison.

- *Decline of bus services*: fall-off of bus ridership of 22 per cent between 1985 and 1995, found by the Commons Select Committee on Transport to be an outcome of deregulation, with a further fall of 2.5 per cent between 1996 and 1999. This makes routes to marginal, low-income communities less viable, causing fares to increase and route infrequencies (Bonnel, 1995).

That these trends have influenced prospects for local retailing is obvious, but the influences are mixed, as Table 6 demonstrates. This highlights the complexity of solutions to the challenge of achieving social inclusion and sustainability in retail regeneration.

Table 6 Supermarkets in regeneration areas: no one right answer?

Advantages	Disadvantages
Offers cheaper food and household goods, and a range of in-store shops such as chemists, newsagents, fishmonger, etc. Cheaper food could reduce food poverty.	Can kill off traders that have been valued members of the local retail community for many years.
Offers a wider choice of goods within the community itself, rather than at a distance which may require expensive journeys.	A large supermarket will not be local to all the residents. Housing over 300 metres away from a store is not considered to be within walking distance. With contraction of other retailers, distance to nearest store may be increased which will disadvantage the more vulnerable such as the elderly, disabled and young mothers.
Provides valuable employment in new store.	Damages employment levels in stores and markets put out of business.
A widened catchment area fosters retail vitality and supports the increased product range available to local residents.	Widened catchments attract more car traffic into area, reducing environmental quality and contributing to air pollution.
Investment gives confidence to an area and can reduce or even do away with stigma.	Danger of community becoming over-dependent on one store.
If located in well-designed retail centre, can draw in customers and increase footfall, which can benefit a range of other shops. Can bring modern facilities and high quality environmental improvements to an area.	If located in a poorly designed site, customers may drive to the supermarket and drive away without making use of any other shops or facilities in the neighbourhood.

3 Key lessons and issues

If there is a lesson to arise from the 14 case studies, it is that there is no one right answer as to how to achieve retail regeneration. The case studies are notable for their diversity of approach – for example, similar 1960s' precincts, demolished in Leeds and Sunderland, have been refurbished in projects in Edinburgh and Glasgow. One case study, Seacroft Green, includes a 110,000 square feet superstore; another, Bradbury Street, has little kiosks which provide a low-risk entry point into the retail sector for budding entrepreneurs.

Key lessons of success

Whatever their diversity, where retail regeneration initiatives are successful, they have factors in common, including:

- *attention to the retail marketplace*: clear attention to what is possible within the framework of the local or sub-regional retail marketplace and available catchment, overlaid with strong aspirations to business success and profitability

- *leadership*: clear leadership in the regeneration initiative

- *involving residents*: respect for local residents' needs and aspirations

- *local vision*: a strong, positive vision for local quality of life, with the retail strategy embedded in the local regeneration or neighbourhood strategy

- *organisational innovation*: control frequently delegated from the local authority to a regeneration company with strong private sector participation or to an experienced community organisation

- *use of investment*: use of public and social investment to reinforce potential achievement in the marketplace, but not to subsidise marginal schemes

- *environment and community facilities*: promotion of the locality as a high quality destination, and thus footfall, through environmental enhancements and community facilities.

Where projects have been less successful, they have:

- *short-term aspirations*: that dominate development planning

- *lack of vision and strategy*: pursuing partnership without achieving a clear vision and consensus on future aspirations, and thus a clear, agreed strategy

- *failure to work towards sustainability*: ignoring the need to achieve economic, social and environmental objectives simultaneously, which defines the term 'sustainable' development.

The remainder of the chapter examines in more detail key lessons and issues suggested by the achievements and limitations of the case studies.

Retail strategy issues

Retail viability and vitality lie at the heart of retail regeneration. Public subsidy can temporarily support initiatives, for example, by release of land at below market cost or by capital investment in environmental improvements, but subsidy can provide only a short-term boost to retail viability. Ultimately, shops stand or fall in terms of profitability in the marketplace, and the health of shopping areas rests on the combined health of their shops. Each of the case studies details the ways and means that regeneration initiatives have supported retail viability by:

- providing shop units of appropriate sizes to both market and retailer needs, ranging from market stalls in Hulme, to small kiosks in Castlemilk and Hackney, to giant superstores, such as at Seacroft

- providing a quality environment

- increasing footfall through location of social and community facilities in the shopping area

- marketing, such as for Green Street.

Extension of catchment area

Beyond serving an existing catchment area, a number of case studies have demonstrated the advantages of increasing catchment. There are three ways to do so. One approach is to reorganise retail facilities, so that they are visible, attractive and appear a secure, pleasant destination to passing non-residents. This is the approach taken at Hulme, where the new food superstore was located on a busy main road leading from the city centre to the suburbs. Access needs to be obvious and straightforward, and car parking secure.

A second approach is to complement the above with provision of retail facilities that fill unmet market opportunities. This usually involves developing a larger superstore, serving a sub-regional catchment. This is the approach taken by Tesco at Seacroft and J. Sainsbury at Castle Vale. In both cases, the retailers committed themselves to providing employment benefits to residents, who also appreciate the larger-format stores available to them.

Developing a marketing strategy

Another means of increasing catchment is to develop a marketing strategy. At one level, such as for new shopping centres, this is about publicising their arrival. But a more sophisticated approach is required for existing, if revamped

Seacroft Green in Leeds, with an extended catchment, represents a major investment in a stigmatised area and a source of local employment. But the increased flow of cars to such developments raises environmental concerns.

facilities. This is the case for the Borough Market and for Green Street. Because of decline in its wholesale function, Borough Market is reinventing itself as a quality farmers' market, and has organised food fairs, theatre events and a website to promote its new position.

At Green Street, the marketing campaign repositions it as a significant regional destination for Asian goods. This involved the use of Single Regeneration Budget (SRB) funds spread over seven years for marketing, co-ordinated by a council officer with experience in media and visitor promotion working with local traders' associations. The innovative use of advertising is described in the case study.

While not every retail destination can define unique characteristics such as Green Street's large number of Asian shops, it demonstrates four points. First, that any destination which finds itself in decline needs to think strategically about its options, and secure professional advice as necessary. Second, that any factor that can distinguish a retail destination, such as a farmers' market, or specialist ethnic foods, or even local architecture and 'café culture', can foster retail vitality if marketed carefully to an appropriate audience. Third, that regeneration funding can be used successfully for marketing. Fourth, that marketing (as at Green Street) and promotion (as at Borough) can be both successful and fun. Fifth, that local councils can assist retail regeneration with provision of expert marketing advice.

Using kiosk units as stepping-stones into the marketplace

Many initiatives provide premises for mainly chain retailers; fewer encourage local entrepreneurship. At the opposite end of the spectrum from the superstore, Castlemilk and Bradbury Street demonstrate that small retail premises in the form of kiosks can provide an opportunity for business start-up. Bradbury Street's ten kiosks provide a starting point for retailers without commitment to the high rents and rates which frequently undermine retail start-ups. The kiosks consist of prefabricated units. Rents are around £55 a week, with an inbuilt 'failure clause' which allows tenants whose business isn't working successfully to get out quickly before debilitating debts are incurred. Conversely, if businesses do well, owners can 'stepping-stone' into the commercial world by renting shops available from the same non-profit organisation.

Supporting vulnerable retail businesses

Business support for vulnerable and aspiring local retailers is a logical feature of the Bradbury Street initiative which could be emulated elsewhere. Prospective tenants of their shops and workspaces make their business plans available to small business experts prior to letting. These are vetted with a requirement to demonstrate that necessary market research has been done to give a reasonable chance of success. For the letting period, additional support is available. This helps business owners secure market position, review investment options and head off financial difficulties. HCD's (Hackney Co-operative Developments) record in the development of businesses that have 'moved on' to commercial premises indicates the benefits of the approach.

Vulnerable position of traditional markets

Case studies suggest a vulnerability of traditional markets. They are frequently much

Kiosk unit at Bradbury Street, Hackney provides local entrepreneurs with a low-risk entry into the retail marketplace with a modest, but commercial, rent and business support.

appreciated by nearby residents for their low prices and good value. However, if they are within covered structures, those structures may well be unsound and require major investment which local authorities do not have available. One option is to let the market run down to the point of closure; another, if the land is at all valuable, is to close the market and sell on the land, thus realising a capital receipt for the local authority. Either way, the market does not survive. Given the historic role of such markets, there is a case for 'listing' to preserve their function. Street markets, on public right of ways, are less vulnerable.

Regeneration strategy and design issues

Refurbishment or demolition?

A major decision is whether to refurbish existing facilities, or demolish and rebuild. Where property is in single ownership, such as a local authority-owned shopping precinct, or just a few hands, both are options. There are advantages and disadvantages, discussed below.

For example, existing centres have been retained at Muirhouse and Castlemilk. On the other hand, Seacroft and Pennywell are examples of demolition of property mainly in single ownership, on the same site in the former, and near the previous site in the latter. Conversely, where there is multiple ownership, as in parades of shops at Upperthorpe or Southey Avenue, or in a typical high street such as Ferndale, refurbishment is usually the only realistic option. Compulsory purchase can also be used to 'buy out' long leases of shopkeepers, as at Seacroft.

Retention of existing shopping precincts

Communities in regeneration areas frequently have a strong sense of community spirit, and residents may have a lingering affection for the local shopping area. This is especially true where it is the social gathering point and focus to an estate, where crime and disorder are not at such levels as to make the centre unviable, and where numbers of residents have not declined precipitously. In these cases, such as Muirhouse, the first choice of residents may be for retention of an existing centre, even though its initial design may be unsuitable for current requirements. However, compared to demolition, retrofitting a shopping precinct and keeping it operational during the process represents a major challenge.

Advantages to retention include continuation of existing social spaces and a sense of continuity for residents during the upheaval of regeneration. These spaces, compared to modern shopping centres, are frequently permeable, that is, they are easily approached on foot from around the neighbourhood. Retained centres are also frequently surrounded by social facilities, from libraries and job centres to offices of local community organisations.

Retention can also help safeguard viability of small, independent retailers, and market stalls with modest turnovers, whose businesses tend not to survive the lengthy transition to new expensive premises. In a number of cases of demolition, such as Seacroft and Hulme, informants expressed concern over small businesses disappearing during regeneration.

There are also constraints in retention, particularly relevant to 1960s'-style precincts: poor design, poor structure and 'non-defensible' space. Outdated designs can be difficult to retrofit. The overall centre or individual units may be of unsuitable size for the existing marketplace – this can mean vacant units which are a drag on repositioning the image of a stigmatised neighbourhood.

Internal arrangements may also be unsuitable. In both Muirhouse and Castlemilk, for example, while shops facing outward are easier to let, shops facing onto enclosed arcades remain difficult to let. These internal spaces are also difficult to clean. Outdated structures also present problems, with common complaints including structural deterioration and leaky roofs. There are also problems with poor delivery arrangements from lorries, which now tend to be much larger than when the centres were built.

Finally, retained shopping centres tend to present difficulty in improving public safety and minimising the influence of substance abusers. This is because these centres tend to have more 'nooks and crannies', which are difficult to police. Existing centres are more likely to retain pubs, which, while serving positive social functions, also attract persons whose behaviour is incompatible with needs of shoppers. The case studies do demonstrate that proactive shopping centre management can reduce these problems.

Demolition and rebuild as an option

A number of case studies involved rebuilding of existing centres including Pennywell, Seacroft and Hulme, and Crown Street, which recreated a neighbourhood shopping environment of shops under new, tenemental flats. Although there are disadvantages in terms of loss of a community's physical centre, there are major advantages to this approach.

The first is that outdated, stigmatised shopping areas are swept aside in one go, replaced by new premises suited to the current retail environment. At a minimum, this has meant premises which are easier to maintain and police, and which have a layout and balance of unit sizes appropriate to the market. In Crown Street, this has been achieved in the context of the re-creation of a traditional urban neighbourhood well suited to its inner city location. The shops in turn have made the new social rented and owner-occupied housing more attractive, contributing to repopulation of the neighbourhood and to objectives of income and tenure diversity of residents.

Important from a retail perspective, Pennywell, Seacroft and Hulme have all broadened their catchments, improving viability. Pennywell, for example, has created an area-wide destination from what was a small, decrepit centre, with a car park busy with vehicles coming into an estate which a few years ago was considered the 'car crime capital' of Europe.

In addition to vitality, there are other advantages to rebuilding. First, local residents have access to bright, clean shops and a broader product range. Second, as volumes of customers increase, public transport can become more viable. Seacroft, for example, is a hub of bus routes, not only into Leeds but also to outlying towns. This increases accessibility for non-car-owning residents. Third, retail centres can go hand-in-hand with community facilities, which increase footfall and community benefits. At Pennywell, the new health and community centre attracts a stream of residents to the first local doctor and dental surgeries to be opened in many years, as part of a healthy living centre. At Seacroft, Tesco, working closely with the local training centre, is providing more than 240 jobs.

There are some disadvantages. In Pennywell and Seacroft, the standard of urban design tends to be poor, producing no more than American-looking, suburban-style shopping centres. Both are 'L'-shaped designs, which are dictated by the anchor retailer, and the main feature is shops facing a car park. Both centres resolutely turn their backs on the surrounding neighbourhood, appearing more like fortresses, with rear sides impenetrable to residents who must walk around to the car park to enter. However, the design makes both car and shopper security more viable, so the trade-off may be considered acceptable. But, if higher standards of urban design were applied uniformly to all shopping malls, greater flows of benefits could be achieved without diminishing retail viability or shopper security.

Shopping parade and high street revitalisation

Where a high street is the historic centre of a neighbourhood or a parade of shops in multiple

Parade of shops restored from a near-derelict condition by a neighbourhood organisation in Longley, Sheffield. A community-owned shop is complemented by a new café, offices for local organisations and private businesses.

ownership is not easy to rationalise, revitalisation is often the preferred option. The case studies indicate that retail vitality can be reinforced in existing high streets but this remains a challenge, given retail trends documented earlier. In this sense, local high street revitalisation (as opposed to city centre) represents a major national challenge, in that, for every high street improving its retail function, there are thousands of others in decline.

Case studies at Longley, Upperthorpe, Bradbury Street and Ferndale demonstrate how concerted effort can support retailing, linked to community facilities, business support and 'place marketing', in the context of a multi-dimensional regeneration strategy. Another common factor is that, in each initiative, a non-profit community organisation leads regeneration.

An exciting redevelopment option is the creation of a whole new high street. This has been undertaken in Crown Street, Glasgow and Hulme, Manchester. Crown Street serves mainly a local catchment, with a new shopping street and mixed tenure housing development within traditional city streetscape patterns. The result is a new 'urban village'.

Hulme is also unique, in that a new high street, just under construction, is 'anchored' by a new food superstore in a small mall, which faces a main road. The physical 'bridge' between mall and the parallel high street is a covered and open marketplace. As in Glasgow, shops in the high street will be at street level with three- and four-storey flats over. Although the case study questions the urban design quality of the mini-mall, and its car dependence, Hulme nevertheless represents an innovative

New, high quality townscape created on brownfield land at Crown Street, Glasgow. New shops are under traditional tenemental-style buildings, with careful attention to streetscape.

approach to new facilities, to broadened catchment and to linking mall development to the concept of a new high street.

Phasing of regeneration and housing policy

The phasing of regeneration, especially demolition of housing in the catchment area and the decanting of population, can have a major impact on the viability of existing retailing, especially shops operating at the margins of profitability. Housing policies that concentrate low-income households in ever fewer estates also have a negative impact. Too often, the case studies show that demolition of a shopping precinct has resulted in the almost complete loss of retailers who go out of business, retire or relocate elsewhere.

Regeneration programmes that wish to retain existing retailers need to consider the impact of the phasing of housing demolition and other aspects of regeneration. In Castle Vale, for example, attention was paid to retaining retailers and easing the transition for community organisations located in the precinct. This included the construction of a 'transition block' attached to the new shopping centre, offering lower rents than the new centre, for businesses that could not afford higher, proposed rents, and a transfer location for community organisations.

The role of community, health and social facilities

The best neighbourhood centres, lively and with ample footfall, combine retail provision with a range of community and health facilities, including libraries, healthy living centres, employment centres and so on. The social focus is a complement to retailing, and both reinforce the sense of destination and 'place' which underpins retail vitality and serves community needs. At Muirhouse, for example, a new arts centre and garden, and new library, provide a social dimension greatly appreciated by local residents. At Pennywell, the new centre shares its site with a healthy living centre, which provides services never before available in the estate. At Green Street, a community educational facility in a refurbished historic building run by the local college is an important local destination facing the high street, and serving social needs. The same is true of a renovated chapel at the heart of the high street in Ferndale. Finally, Bradbury Street provides workspaces above shops, which increase the flow of people in the area.

The quality of public space is also important. Green Street has not only widened its pavements and provided seating areas for shoppers, it has also commissioned local people, young and old, to prepare pavement mosaics. Bradbury Street hopes to take this a step further, by creating a new civic square in Hackney. On the other side of the coin, some developments, such as at Seacroft, have created little in the way of quality public or social space, and their retail achievement, although substantial, seems limited by this.

Community and Health Resource Project next to the Pennywell Shopping Centre brings a range of community benefits, including the first on-estate surgery, and increases footfall for the centre

Environmental issues

Improving environmental benefits

Most of the case studies report local environmental improvements, some of high quality:

- new building and quality urban design (Crown Street, Bradbury Street)

- restoration of historic (Ferndale, Green Street, Borough Market) and other buildings (Upperthorpe, Longley and Bradbury Street)

- improved streetscape (Green Street, Crown Street)

- new market hall (Hulme)

- innovation in retail facilities (kiosks at Bradbury Street and Castlemilk).

Good new developments contribute to the quality of urban neighbourhoods, discussed below. Aside from their social benefits, recycling of old and historic buildings saves substantial amounts of 'embodied' energy involved in building demolition and construction.

Fostering good urban design

Good urban design is vital to sustainability, particularly for inner city neighbourhoods hoping to redress population decline and convince potential residents that higher density urban living can mean a high quality of life. Most impressive from an urban design point of view are the new neighbourhoods in Crown Street and Hulme. On the other side of the coin, the middling quality of urban design in some new shopping centres is also noted, deriving from security requirements, particularly for

shoppers' cars, and from a perceived need by retailers to keep costs down by use of common site development patterns, store envelopes and servicing arrangements around the country.

Comparison of the best and the most mediocre of building and site designs, and the national perspective of the retail food chains that control 70 per cent of the market, suggests that national retail site design guidance would be of benefit in improving the general quality of retail development. This could be prepared on behalf of DETR and used as a tool of planning policy in assessing retail planning applications. There is no reason why the quality of urban design for new retail premises and sites cannot be substantially improved to the level of the country's better designs. Not to do so leaves a legacy of mediocre buildings and tin sheds, many of which could still be with us in 50 years. Although it is appreciated that retailers, particularly discount retailers who serve disadvantaged communities, want to opt for least-cost developments, it is also the case that any guidance that applies to all retailers across the board will have only relative effects.

Expanded catchments and nil achievement of traffic reduction and CO_2 emissions

Although fewer, larger stores with expanded catchments clearly generate retail vitality, these expanded catchments are always predicated on attracting car-borne shoppers from further afield. This contributes to the unhealthy cycle of more car use, more pollution and so on. A glaring omission in initiatives documented here is signal failure to make any attempt to reduce traffic volumes or to address the issue of the increase in CO_2 emissions and other pollutants caused by the very success of developments predicated on more cars bringing more shoppers. Indeed, as noted in the first chapter, the poor quality of most public transport reinforces the common perception that car use is the *sine qua non* of a prosperous lifestyle and that retail vitality and increased car use have to go hand in hand.

A few local authorities are making an effort, Manchester's and Sheffield's trams being a case in point. Seacroft has a busy bus station located immediately in front of the new Tesco. Although these demonstrate that some things can be done locally, for most initiatives, car use is not an issue which can be resolved at the local level. Under current conditions, and despite the intentions of PPG 6, local action to stem increases in car use can only disadvantage retail regeneration – where car use for shopping is encouraged by investments in new roads, inadequate alternatives and by failure to address the issue of lack of parking charges at shopping malls. Changes can only come from national commitment and policy:

1 to establish targets for national CO_2 reductions that can be applied at regional and local levels

2 to link transport and land use decisions to energy policy to work towards those targets and to provide a spatial framework for local action

3 to establish a system of environmental impact assessment for retail developments

4 to have a concerted national effort to improve public transport, and make walking and cycling an alternative, so that car use is a less favoured option.

Organisational and social issues

Quality of partnership

Most of the cases reviewed here involved partnership between council, retailers, developers, training organisations, residents and other stakeholders. Considerable research has been done on partnership and these lessons hold here (Carley *et al.*, 2000a). However, some points stand out.

Retail revival is a specialist area, requiring market knowledge and ability to respond quickly to fluid market conditions. This meant that an effective partnership model was one in which the local authority was an equal partner rather than lead agency. In partnerships intending large retail premises, and major investments, supermarkets and/or developers played a significant role in decision processes in two ways.

The first was confined mainly to specification of physical requirements which allowed premises to be rented quickly. This is important because quick rental is tangible proof of regeneration and reduction of the stigma that dogs many of these areas. Beyond this, although many retail partners provide valuable advice, they tend not to be deeply interested in partnership processes, preferring to focus on retailing. Castlemilk and Muirhouse are examples. For many retailers, it is unreasonable to expect much in the way of active involvement.

The second type of involvement is active role in partnership, leading to a broader range of achievements including employment benefits, as at Seacroft and Castle Vale. In the latter, the supermarket also plays a significant management role in the retail centre. In

Castlemilk, the centre owner has played the major role in its regeneration, investing nearly £5 million pounds in what was one of Scotland's most deprived estates. This is in accord with the owner's organisational culture, but they are also trading at a profit. It demonstrates what is possible when owners are encouraged and enabled to become committed.

There is a sense of tension in some larger partnerships, with retailers and/or developers who are expected to commit major amounts of investment wanting to call the shots, compared with community representatives and existing small traders who feel excluded from deliberations dictated by market considerations. The best solution appears in the structure of partnership, which provides a substantive role for community organisations to participate and learn about the 'ins and outs' of development options, and to make their views known. It is also important that local authorities, and community and training organisations, are in a position to work together to ensure that decisions on retail investments also produce a flow of benefits to the local community. An effective chairperson of the regeneration partnership will ensure that all stakeholders have a sense of inclusion in discussion and decision making, which then represents a consensus on strategy.

Larger regeneration partnerships, with major multi-functional programmes, tend to operate most effectively through retail sub-groups, which enable specialist expertise to be applied as necessary. Almost always, an organisational mechanism evolves which allows the partnership to operate at arm's-length, and in a more focused fashion, than local authority decision structures normally allow. North Edinburgh Area Regeneration, Hulme Regeneration and Pride in Pennywell are examples.

Management and training issues

Managing for public safety

Public safety and anti-social behaviour are vital issues for many initiatives discussed here. The solutions tend to be straightforward. Litter and graffiti need to be cleaned promptly. In Pennywell, for example, the local council agreed quickly to a twice-a-day litter clean-up when it became apparent that once a day was not enough. At Muirhouse, the shopping centre management is able to call out specialist contractors to remove graffiti on a daily basis.

For security, CCTV is a favoured option, but the lesson is that it must be monitored and provision must be made for addressing problems as they arise. This requires finance and proactive management. In Pennywell, it was found that security personnel needed to be available on a 24-hour-per-day, seven-day-per-week schedule to meet requirements.

Training and local employment

A significant finding is that, in the few cases where retailers set out to provide employment opportunities for the long-term unemployed, they were successful in doing so. This suggests that employment schemes have potential to reduce unemployment, particularly as the 'sequential' land use test makes inner city, brownfield sites more attractive.

A key lies with employers working closely with a local, experienced training organisation and other stakeholders, including the Employment Service, providing training, literacy and numeracy courses and child care, as necessary. Seacroft, Hulme and Castle Vale are cases where employment benefits are reported. At Braehead, there were less employment benefits than anticipated, despite the size of the development, because of the slow response of the public agencies involved. This was related to the development's location on brownfield land on the border of a number of jurisdictions with differing boundaries.

The emergence of the service sector as a major source of employment in the 1990s suggests that more local authorities should look to job creation for the long-term unemployed as an element in retail development on brownfield sites.

Issues of concern to local authorities

Phasing of attention to retail decline

Despite the relative success in retail regeneration reported here, the likelihood is that these cases are exceptions rather than the rule. For every regeneration programme, there are other shopping centres slipping into decline – almost inevitable given the retail trends documented earlier. There is concern that regeneration programmes are 'too little, too late' in targeting mainly areas which have already experienced significant decline and when the task is then very substantial.

Although action by local authorities on declining retail areas outside of regeneration areas may be limited by resources, an appropriate response is to monitor retail viability in neighbourhood and district areas. Early action to counter decline could then be taken while it is cost-effective to do so, following, for example, from the type of initiatives used successfully in Green Street, Bradbury Street and other locations; and used

successfully in city centre management initiatives (Boots the Chemists and Civic Trust, 1996). Within the context of community planning, local organisations could also be empowered to do more to help retail vitality, working with shopkeepers to enhance the shopping environment.

At the level of the local authority, retail and neighbourhood centre improvement strategies can be prioritised by establishment of a hierarchy of shopping areas and responses to their development needs. This is the approach that is being taken by Rhondda Cynon Taff Council which has Objective 1 status and a forward planning framework for retail improvement among other development options. It has established three levels of retail function and is devising support and participation plans applicable to each level. The local community development trust in Ferndale, working with the local councillor, is anticipating this opportunity and has requested funding to undertake its own forward planning and retail enhancement study. This is important, not only because such a study is being undertaken, but also because local people and traders with local knowledge are both inputting to the study and taking subsequent ownership of it. Discussions with shopkeepers in Ferndale suggest pent-up demand for local participation, but also the need to re-establish and support a local traders' organisation.

Use of rate variation as a tool of policy[1]

Rates are at best a minor issue for larger retailers and national chains who build costs into pricing structures and offset variations between locations. However, for small retailers in regeneration areas and elsewhere, the level of rates is an important consideration in retail viability. Some businesses in this study questioned why they should pay the same rates as premises located within wealthy areas. Others felt that some opportunity for tapering rates would provide small businesses with an opportunity to start up on a healthy footing. Similarly, the introduction of a 'rates holiday' when a business is in trouble was seen to be preferable to being forced out of business when unable to meet combined rent and rates demands.

The Green Paper *Modernising Local Government* discusses provision of rate relief in deprived areas, suggested in the Urban Task Force report. This recommended that small businesses would be entitled to rate reductions with the cost being met through the national rate pool rather than having to be funded by individual authorities. The potential for rate relief was also reviewed in PAT 13. While it supported rate relief as a way to sustain shops in deprived areas, it noted that rents and consequently rates were often already low in such areas. Relief might therefore have limited impact on market viability. However, profit margins for local shops in regeneration areas are often very low so even modest relief could make a difference between a shop remaining or closing. Reduced rates could also help nurture rentals in vacant shops.

There is precedent in an existing rate relief scheme for village shops and post offices in rural areas, implemented in 1998. This gives 50 per cent mandatory relief for any sole general store (selling food) or post office in settlements with a population of less than 3,000 and with a rateable value of less than £6,000. Local authorities have the discretionary power to increase the rate relief to 100 per cent and to allow relief to any other business in such settlements considered vital to the community. This is subject to a rateable value of £12,000. Central government funds the full cost of the mandatory rate relief and 75 per cent of the discretionary relief. The purpose is to protect the last providers of essential services in isolated rural communities.

Research suggests that the mandatory rate relief scheme is working (Local Government Association, unpublished). Local authorities are experiencing more difficulties administering the discretionary scheme, particularly where preference has to be given to one business over another. This difficulty would likely increase in urban areas where there is a diverse range of businesses and overlapping catchment areas.

Research demonstrates that there is a relationship between changes in business rates and rents and that increases in non-domestic rents result in lower property rents (Institute for Fiscal Studies, 1995). Similarly, the value of rate relief may be offset over time by rent increases. This raises the concern that benefits of rate relief would tend to be short term and erode over time, as the market adapts to different conditions and costs.

4 Refurbishing existing local shopping centres and high streets

Existing local shopping precincts

MUIRHOUSE SHOPPING CENTRE, EDINBURGH

Refurbishment of 1960s' local shopping precinct on Edinburgh peripheral estate.

Key points
- Step-by-step approach to task of reinforcing a neighbourhood centre important to residents.
- Better security to address tension between shoppers and substance abusers.
- Vulnerability of the centre's retail vitality and regeneration programme from proposed nearby development of large supermarket.

Synopsis

As well as an important retail facility, the shopping centre is a social hub for the community. Responding to residents' aspirations for improving the existing centre, rather than demolition, the initiative is making progress against constraints, which include the challenge of retrofitting a 1960s'-style precinct, multiple ownership and little market opportunity to establish a wider catchment in an area well provided with large supermarkets. In urban design terms, the existing centre remains accessible from all sides, with a new library, arts facilities and community business centre.

The shopping centre was constructed in 1968 on a new estate consisting of tenements and high-rises. There is major investment in new social housing and low-cost homes for sale. Although pleasantly overlooking the sea, the estate was synonymous with social problems, especially substance abuse, providing the location for the film *Trainspotting*. Muirhouse sits within Greater Pilton, home to around 16,000 persons. Regeneration is carried out by North Edinburgh Area Regeneration (NEAR), a long-standing partnership.

The shopping centre, serving a local catchment, remains in council ownership, but with a long head lease of the retail premises (but not the public areas) to the estate developer, the Boland Group. The centre consists of 30 retail units, with a supermarket, pub and four-storey flats above the shops. Although these provide

custom, they also make refurbishment difficult because shops' walls provide support to the structure above. Around four-fifths of the retail units are occupied and there is still reasonable trade for a baker, fruiterer, butcher, chemist, off-licence, hair salon, takeaways and other businesses.

Historically, the centre traded on a healthy basis until the mid-1980s, for food and convenience goods but also fashion and shoes. This latter type of retailer started closing in the late 1980s. The result, according to Boland, was loss of a 'critical mass' of shop numbers and variety, and footfall. Retail viability also suffered from demolition of surrounding housing units as part of regeneration, which reduced household numbers in the catchment, and from an increasing concentration of poor households, causing decline in average annual income.

The refurbishment process started in 1994 when residents identified the centre's poor condition as a concern. For professionals, demolition seemed an option. However, a residents' survey found strong allegiance to the centre, particularly for households without cars – alternative shops being out of walking range. The centre is said to be a 'collective corner store'. Half of residents questioned used Muirhouse as their main food shopping centre. Many identified barriers to increased use as substance abusers and dirty, rundown appearance.

A decision was made to retain the existing centre – to provide continuity for residents and traders during improvement. The design solutions included enclosing a pedestrianised off-street mall with a roof/entrance portico, tree planting, new pavements, new road link and angle parking to encourage passing trade. Organisationally, a Muirhouse Shopping Centre Management Association has been established, of stakeholders including NEAR, the Council, Boland Group and representatives of resident and tenants' associations with the police in an advisory capacity.

The shopping centre is being refurbished in a joint venture between the public sector and Boland. Other investments include a new library, a community arts centre and café, and community business centre. The refurbishments, about one-half completed, have improved retail viability in the areas of the centre facing the street but, in the 'mall', there are still vacant units. Once the mall has lockable doors and a regular 9.00 p.m. closure, the intention is to encourage voluntary organisations to make use of this area. One unit is let to an IT skills centre, set up by the local college in association with Deutsche Bank.

Points of inspiration

- *Reinforcing a neighbourhood centre*: local residents felt the existing centre was important to them and deserved improvement. In addition to retail improvements, the initiative is drawing together funding streams to cement this focus. This includes a proposed Community Tower in a hard-to-let block of flats, being taken forward by the leading community organisation, the Pilton Partnership (PP). This will provide shared office premises for voluntary organisations currently scattered around Greater Pilton. The PP has established a community asset management organisation, which will take over the building.

- *Personal security*: a primary task was to address loitering substance abusers. A concierge system was started, hiring local residents with training provided free by the Council's Housing Department. A closed-circuit television (CCTV) system was installed, monitored by the concierges, with the assistance of the police. Finally, if problems persist, the Council is prepared to consider a by-law making it illegal to consume alcohol in the centre.

- *Taking a step-by-step approach*: compared to wholesale demolition, retrofitting a precinct and keeping it operational represents a major challenge. NEAR has taken a step-by-step approach, trying out initiatives and gradually improving both the environment and the trading position of the shopping centre. In the absence of

Layout of the Muirhouse Shopping Centre shows the new community facilities clustered around the centre.

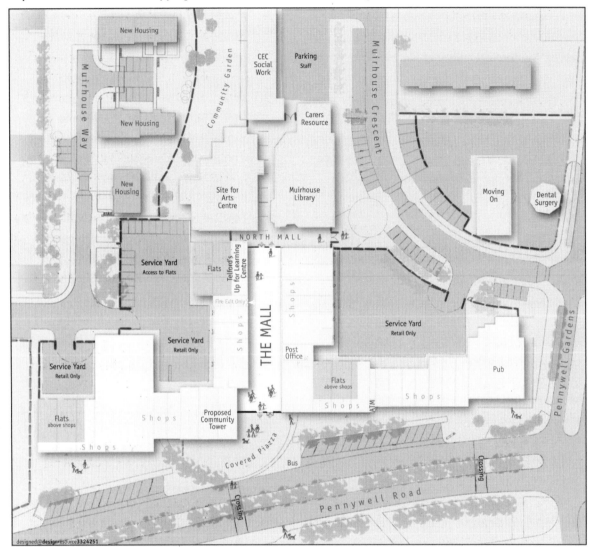

opportunity to extend the catchment, footfall is to be increased by concentrating public services, voluntary organisations and start-up businesses.

Constraints on regeneration

- *Weak partnership*: as for many retail initiatives, the partnership is weak. There is no traders' association and individual traders have demonstrated little

willingness to attend meetings. Community representatives, on the other hand, attend frequently but don't always feel decisions go their way. The head leaseholder of the retail shop units is unhappy with the covered mall as a design solution, which they feel creates a poor quality interior space in a public right of way. This, they suggest, will be difficult to clean and police. They also feel that the Council's commitment to cleansing in the centre is less than necessary.

- *Planning and location of competition*: the trading position of the centre's Kwik Save is just within the commercially viable but, if planning permission is given for a proposed Asda Wal-Mart nearby, the centre's viability could be undermined. Kwik Save suggests that, if this occured, it would close its Muirhouse store. It is unlikely that any other supermarket chain would step in. Generally, the Council admits that North Edinburgh is close to having too many food supermarkets.

- *Need for rates relief*: both regeneration practitioners and the leaseholder find it disturbing that rates are set by reference to notional rental returns for similar-sized shops elsewhere in Edinburgh, when 'there is virtually no market for shops in this location, some of which have been vacant for eight years'. They feel it is not cost-effective to spend public money on environmental improvements when the rating structure weakens retail viability in marginal trading areas. Currently, in their view, rate demands on the centre make it a negative asset, which they support mainly because of company goodwill.

CASTLEMILK SHOPPING CENTRE, GLASGOW

Refurbishment, with rebuilding, of local shopping precinct on Glasgow peripheral estate, mainly funded by the owner.

Key points

- Private shopping centre operator working with the local community giving good relationship between the shopping centre manager and local groups, and affordable rents rather than vacant units.
- Small kiosk units enliven the entrance and provide low-cost space for local entrepreneurs.
- Retrofitting an existing centre with arcade leaves internal areas difficult to let, compared with visible external shop units.

Synopsis

This 55-unit shopping centre provides the physical and social focal point to a peripheral estate which once housed 37,000 persons and is now home to around 12,000. It consists of a covered central arcade surrounded by three outward-facing shopping frontages. The centre is managed by a private company on a long-lease basis, and they are committed to the community. They have recently made substantial investments as part of an overall regeneration programme. In 1997, the frontage was demolished and replaced by a new purpose-built food store. Reorganising the space has created a new sense of vitality along this frontage, but internal shopping spaces remain difficult to let.

Castlemilk was designated one of four Scottish Urban Partnerships in 1988. In its response to an early strategy, the community-based Castlemilk Umbrella Group (1989) highlighted a number of 'crunch issues' including the proposal that the existing shopping centre be considered 'a town centre not just a shopping centre'. To meet this requirement, the community proposed integrating retail functions with community projects.

A survey found that 96 per cent of residents saw the development of the shopping centre as a key issue with half citing the shopping centre as Castlemilk's 'worst feature'. Although the Council owned the land, the building is on long-term lease to a private company, Estates and Agency Holdings, which also manages the centre. In 1995, Estates and Agency Holdings carried out a £1m upgrading as part of phased regeneration.

In 1997, as part of a complicated development arrangement involving properties elsewhere in the city, Estate and Agency Holdings invested £4.5m in a major redevelopment involving partial demolition, relocation of the car park to the front of the centre and development of a new supermarket,

leased to Kwik Save. Funding for New Life ended in 1995, although the area continued to receive limited funding as a newly designated Social Inclusion Partnership (SIP) area.

Points of inspiration

- *Relationship with the community*: the centre operator markets the centre as 'for the community'. Its viability is due in part to the personal initiative of the manager in getting involved in community initiatives, including health and community safety initiatives. In addition, both major tenants, Iceland and Kwik Save, see themselves as playing a community role, building customer loyalty. Kwik Save, for instance, works alongside a Healthy Castlemilk project to provide a pensioners' voucher scheme towards wholesome food purchases.

- *Business development*: the kiosk units have proved popular with modest local businesses looking to set up with minimum overheads. The kiosks range from 90 to 190 sq. ft with rents from a little over £2,000 to

Renovated mall at the shopping centre in Castlemilk, Glasgow with new kiosk units on the right-hand side.

£4,000 per year. Castlemilk Economic Development Agency (CEDA) is on hand to offer business advice to start-ups.

- *Management and security*: the centre has its share of shoplifting and 'undesirables hanging about' but the introduction of CCTV cameras with 24-hour security has reduced problems to manageable proportions. A commitment to immediate removal of graffiti has proved a deterrent. Although the local chemist is part of the methadone programme, a potentially negative impact is minimised by the chemist's decision to serve a manageable number of clients and close liaison between chemist and GPs.

- *Affordable rents*: the centre operator is willing to negotiate on rent levels, offering 'tapered' rents or rent-free periods, which is seen as a tactic to reduce rates needing to be paid on vacant units and with service charges offsetting rent losses to an extent. These agreements are negotiated independently of the lease by 'side letter' and are not transferable.

Constraints on regeneration

- *Design*: the original centre was developed in the 1960s and is considered to be of poor design, requiring considerable retrofitting to make it workable. Development of the kiosks opposite the main shopping parade has given vitality to this area. An arcade, however, has struggled to attract rental interest with retailers moving out as fast as they move in. The two major food retailers, located at the more viable front, have not helped to generate footfall in the arcade.

- *Loss of business due to redevelopment works and uncertainty*: when first built, the centre traded well and included a number of national chains such as Woolworth's and Boots. However, given that there were early plans to demolish the centre, retailers were allowed to break their leases to minimise compensation payments. Declining local population, high rates of unemployment and growing social problems meant that, in many cases, it was only the lease that held operators. Growing uncertainty surrounding the future of the centre discouraged many retailers from committing to operation in the centre.

- *Persistence of stigma*: the centre's operator employs letting agents to attract retailers. Although there has been some success, there is still much to do in overcoming 'the black name of Castlemilk'. Without increasing the catchment to shoppers from outside the area, the limited spending power of local residents means that attempts to introduce more competition, and hence choice for consumers, negatively impacts on existing businesses' viability.

- *Lack of community facilities*: while recent investment in leisure facilities has benefited footfall, lack of other cultural and community facilities within the centre undermines its status as a 'town centre'. The Partnership is currently in negotiations with the centre management over utilisation of the vacant and upper arcade units for community use.

CASTLE VALE, BIRMINGHAM

Redevelopment of a 1960s' precinct, with new superstore, retail centre, public square and community facilities.

Key points

- J. Sainsbury a full partner in regeneration, committed to local employment benefits; 33 per cent of jobs going to local unemployed residents.
- Shopping centre turned 'inside out' so it faces a main road. Its attraction to passing customers increases catchment, footfall, vitality and the range of facilities available to residents.

Synopsis

A depressed, stigmatised and inward-looking precinct has been transformed into a lively retail and community centre led by a Housing Action Trust (HAT) in partnership with a major supermarket operator.

Castle Vale is the largest post-war estate in Birmingham, with a population of 11,000. It was transferred to a Housing Action Trust (HAT) in 1994. The HAT then embarked on a regeneration programme involving construction of 1,100 new homes and refurbishment of 900 other properties.

While housing improvement was the initial goal, regeneration of the area's 1960s' shopping centre was also within the scope of the HAT. Alongside concern over public safety, half of residents identified poor shopping and poor image of the centre as problems. When the HAT was established, 30 per cent of the centre's 42 retail units were vacant. Shortly after, the centre's key anchor, Kwik Save, moved out.

One problem with the existing design was that the centre was inward looking, had no identifiable frontage from the nearby main thoroughfare and was therefore unable to attract passing trade from neighbouring affluent areas. Turning the centre around substantially increased footfall and ensures a good range of shops for local residents.

The HAT secured freehold to the site in 1996, which it then sold on to J. Sainsbury with income from the sale ploughed back into regeneration. Throughout the redevelopment, the HAT attempted to minimise disruption to residents, traders and community organisations that had used the centre. A free bus service ran to the nearest quality shopping area. A number of existing users were accommodated within a 'relocation block' constructed by J. Sainsbury. Local consultation was a priority and a comprehensive programme to update residents on progress was implemented. The new shopping centre is said to have helped generate community spirit.

The centre was redeveloped in 1999 at a cost of £35 m. – the largest Sainsbury's investment outside London. A 50,000 sq. ft Sainsbury's store opened in 2000 attracting 20,000 customers per week. The scheme also includes smaller retail units, taken up by existing businesses including a chemist, post office, solicitors, bookmaker and dental surgery. The scheme contains a healthy living centre, and public square and public artwork, all with CCTV. In early 2001, the Tenants and Residents Alliance and a One Stop Centre moved in, the latter providing employment, education and training advice.

Throughout the redevelopment, the HAT worked in partnership with J. Sainsbury on a recruitment drive to optimise residents' chances of competing for jobs. Originally, Sainsbury's aimed to fill 15 per cent of 420 jobs with local residents, but the actual number exceeds 33 per cent. A training centre was established to help residents complete application forms and tests.

Points of inspiration

- *Partnership with supermarket operator*: the decision to appoint J. Sainsbury as preferred developer was based on the company's willingness to be a partner in regeneration and to create local employment. The company is represented on the HAT Board and that of the healthy living centre. Taken together, this represents a real commitment to partnership. Once Sainsbury's were on board, they then assumed responsibility for filling the other retail units. Transferring responsibility for management, security and ongoing maintenance to commercial owners ensures that there is no outstanding liability against the public purse.

- *Recycling of capital receipts*: capital receipts generated through the sale of the site were reinvested in the regeneration programme. In addition, a percentage was top-sliced and invested in a charitable Community Fund to help support voluntary sector organisations.

- *Relocation of existing businesses*: there is always a need to balance community needs with commercial reality. A number of traders were relocated into the purpose-built relocation block, designed to offer more affordable rents and rates adjacent to the main centre.

- *Preferential leasing arrangements for community users*: the HAT negotiated on behalf of community users to secure discounted rents. A paid HAT officer works alongside community groups to help them achieve their aspirations and secure realistic funding.

Constraints on regeneration

- *Countering poor image*: difficulties surrounding negotiations with some existing traders led to negative publicity, a problem that bedevilled many HATs. Opposition to the scheme was well organised and high profile. However, the HAT securing a high-profile anchor store in Sainsbury's provided a boost to a deprived area whose supermarket had closed. This helped dispel the HAT's negative image. Sainsbury's use of Castle Vale within its own publicity provides external validation for the scheme.

Existing local parades of shops

SOUTHEY AVENUE, LONGLEY ESTATE, SHEFFIELD

Refurbishment of a parade of largely derelict shops, to give a community-owned store, café and community enterprise centre, and two privately owned shops.

Key points

- Application of community enterprise and use of modest subsidy has transformed shops at the heart of the estate, encouraging private investment in the remaining shops.
- Physical regeneration provides a base for community initiatives, such as a tool bank and housing surgery.
- A community-owned food shop trades only at the margin of viability.

Synopsis

A non-profit community company purchased three of five shops in a derelict parade. The outcome is a new physical hub for the estate, and a social and economic hub for community participation in the estate's regeneration.

Longley comprises 1,850 houses and is part of a broad band of council estates across north-east Sheffield which are home to 42,000 people. Most of the estates have suffered from the decline of traditional industry.

The LOCAL Project in Southey Avenue is a neighbourhood regeneration initiative that has revitalised a parade of disused shops facing a square of four greens in the heart of the estate. The aim of the project is to develop and manage the shops to serve both commercial and social needs of the community and to provide a focal point for regeneration. LOCAL is the Longley Organised Community Association Limited, a company limited by guarantee with membership open to any resident of the estate. Although a limited company, LOCAL has also been recognised by Sheffield Council as the estate's tenants' organisation, which enables it to access a modest tenants' levy for its core funding. This required a shift in stance by the Council towards recognition of community

frameworks outside of traditional models.

Within the project, there is a community owned and managed LOCAL store, a wholly owned trading arm of the project. LOCAL is supported by Sheffield Council and the Sheffield Community Enterprise Development Unit (SCEDU), itself a community enterprise, which assists small businesses and community organisations across the city. SCEDU has a modest financial stake in LOCAL. LOCAL evolved out of the residents' and tenants' association, which needed to establish itself as a legal entity if it was to take ownership of the vacant shops.

The regeneration of the five-shop parade is largely complete. The LOCAL food store is a pilot community-owned retail project operated in conjunction with the wholesaler, Mace, to sell groceries and rent videos. It provides seven jobs, with profits rolled back into the business. Of the two remaining community-owned shops, one is a community café with a meeting room and offices above. The other is the Four Greens Centre, headquarters of LOCAL but also containing a community tool bank for local residents, a housing advice surgery and community offices, including that of the South Yorkshire Housing Association, which provided financial advice and which is a local social landlord. Two other retail units, privately owned, are now lively local businesses, one of which is a hardware store and the other a joinery business. They have been renovated following refurbishment of LOCAL's three units.

Having accomplished its initial intention, LOCAL is looking to a forward strategy to refurbish the greens linked to establishment of a green space maintenance enterprise, establishment of a farmers' market, a wardened housing project and development of better transport links for the estate. It would also like to take a role in estate self-management.

Points of inspiration

- *Use of retail refurbishment as a springboard for community regeneration*: the project has provided an attractive physical hub for the estate, from a 'before' situation of a derelict, boarded-up parade of shops. It also provides a social focus for community enterprise. The formation of LOCAL as a company limited by guarantee provided an organisational means for a community asset base, beginning with the three shops, to develop its competences in a variety of areas of enterprise.

- *Linkage between shop, café and community-managed meeting space*: there are benefits from these relationships in terms of ordering and use of foodstuffs, and opportunities for LOCAL to shift into

other related commercial areas, such as catering.

Constraints on regeneration

- *Viability of the community-owned store*: at this time, the community-owned store is operating at a small loss on a credible turnover of around £600,000 per year. This is not unusual – many small retailers operate near the margins of viability. It is not yet clear whether the community-owned store will remain a viable retail model when it shifts, as it must, to a situation of zero subsidy. It is still finding its feet as of this writing, but, whatever the outcome, there are already benefits in terms of learning about options for community enterprise.

- *Relationships with nearby retailers*: even as the launch of the community-owned shop took place, opened by the Secretary of State for Education, Radio 4 was interviewing nearby shopkeepers who objected to the subsidy going into the LOCAL store, which they felt conferred unfair advantage. LOCAL's argument is that it broadened the range of goods available to the community and lowered prices, which were too high. Relationships have now evolved, to the extent that LOCAL and nearby shopkeepers are now exploring the possibility of group purchasing of wholesale foodstuffs. And, given that local shops are in intense competition with big multiple stores, LOCAL-initiated projects, such as the green refurbishment, could benefit all local retailers by increasing footfall.

BRADBURY STREET, LONDON BOROUGH OF HACKNEY

In a vibrant multi-ethnic neighbourhood, this is a development of shop regeneration, café, managed workspaces and a kiosk initiative by a non-profit development organisation.

Key points

- Ability of locally based voluntary organisation to deliver retail and workspace premises, and local economic and social development.
- Careful management to ensure start-up businesses move to commercial viability, creating opportunities for new start-ups.
- Resistance of local council to neighbourhood management.

Synopsis

Bradbury Street consists of Victorian shops, managed workspaces, community café and ten kiosk units, which provide retail start-up opportunities with minimum risk. Tenancies are commercial, at the lower end of market rent. There is an assumption that businesses will move on, opening up space for new businesses and the support services offered by Hackney Co-operative Developments.

Hackney Co-operative Development's (HCD's) mission is to encourage the start-up and sustainability of local retail and service businesses in Hackney by provision of premises at reasonable rents and business support. HCD is concerned to reverse social exclusion by community economic development and fostering neighbourhood governance.

The site of the development is a city block off the busy Kingsland High Street. The existing, now refurbished, terrace was derelict as a result of an aborted regeneration scheme. HCD's first task was to acquire clear title to the site from a variety of owners, and to renovate the houses for short life, co-operative tenancies.

By 1992, however, renovation of much of the existing Victorian shopping streetscape, with new-build workspaces behind, seemed preferable to demolition. This would make use of a package of regeneration funding. At the same time, the local authority entered into agreement with Peabody Housing to provide social housing at the cleared end of the site. HCD found, through competition, a community-oriented, architectural firm to take forward a striking development of 16 retail units (six shops and ten award-winning kiosks) and 25 workshop and office units opening on to the side of the structure though a new, small public square.

The demand for retail and workspace premises is indicated from the waiting list for units, even though tenants are required to 'move on, with support' when their businesses either become profitable or it becomes obvious they won't make it in the marketplace. Prospective tenants have their business plans and market research vetted. Leases had been up to nine years, but HCD is drawing back to 'easy in/out' two-year, renewable leases for all except the Jazz and Poetry Café, which is on a long-term arrangement. Successful businesses that have moved on include a bike shop, a hairdresser, a children's bookshop and a software firm.

On the retail side, the kiosks provide a safe starting point for new retailers wanting to get started without commitment to the high rents and rates that frequently undermine start-ups. The kiosks consist of 30 sq. m. prefabricated units, with a folding hatch at the front that creates either a window display or counter. There is an inbuilt 'failure clause', which allows tenants whose business isn't working to get out quickly before debilitating debts are incurred. Conversely, if businesses do well, the owners can 'stepping-stone' into the commercial world by renting one of HCD's shops. Currently, kiosk tenants include an African art shop, a hair salon, a 'pound shop' and a dance music stall.

HCD's operating principle is that everything it does must be socially responsible and financially sustainable. HCD currently has 30,000 sq. ft of commercially viable space as an asset base including a new headquarters, which also provides training space for the local college, a theatre group and offices. HCD's broader role includes: identification of community business opportunities within Hackney's diverse population; implementing training and marketing projects for clients; and promoting inter-agency partnerships.

As an example of the latter, HCD has now set its sights on partnership regeneration of the large parking area behind the existing development. A new civic square is proposed, with additional flats, a playground and workspaces, with HCD working with a commercial developer and the Council. The purpose is to demonstrate that the voluntary sector, business and local government can co-operate to create innovative public spaces and local services. In another initiative, HCD is exploring the potential for inter-local business co-operation to deliver commercial and/or social benefits. Joint purchasing arrangements for small food retailers is one example; co-operative recycling is another.

Points of inspiration

- *Voluntary organisation delivers*: Bradbury Street shows that voluntary organisations can deliver local physical, economic and social regeneration. Shops are let to local retailers and workspaces to new businesses – all supported by professional advisers.

- *HCD as a ramp to business success – but not a permanent source of subsidy*: having provided its 41 tenants with the opportunity for a foothold in the marketplace, HCD makes a point of ensuring that it is moving towards independence and profitability. Commercial considerations influence rent levels so that its tenants are operating within a commercial, rather than subsidised, context, but on a low-risk basis while they are learning what works in the marketplace.

- *Kiosks as a starting point*: HCD's kiosks not only provide valuable starter units, but also, taken together, create a striking mini-marketplace for the local community. Their modular prefabrication means they can be replicated as developments move forward on the new civic square.

Renovated terrace and shops in Bradbury Street with the new drum-shaped 'jazz café' under community offices. The managed workspaces are above the shops.

- *IT links tenants and HCD*: the workspaces are linked by an intranet network enabling a full range of electronic communications. This in turn provides these start-up businesses with full access to worldwide networks.

Constraints on regeneration

- *Managing anti-social behaviour and public space*: the creation of new public space brings with it some responsibility for the management of that space to maintain its quality and the commercial viability. In an inner city location, this can mean management of anti-social behaviour, such as drunkenness and littering. There is also a need for community-based management of cultural activities. Currently, there is no clear arrangement between HCD and the local council over who ought to do what, and how, most effectively. Nor is there much willingness as yet, on the part of the Council, to devolve responsibility for neighbourhood management.

Existing high streets

UPPERTHORPE, SHEFFIELD

Regeneration of an inner city high street of shops and community facilities.

Key points

- Leading role of community alliance working with the Council, businesses and other stakeholders.
- Use of SRB funding for premises refurbishment, environmental improvements, traffic calming, and training and job creation.

Synopsis

A small high street which has suffered from a large nearby supermarket and other changes. The retail strategy is based on a consultant's assessment of options, public investment in a refurbished library and baths, and a healthy living centre. Footfall is increased by developing retail and social facilities.

There are currently 23 shop units in mixed ownership in the high street of this village within a long-standing regeneration area. Six are vacant with a number of hot food shops closed during the daytime adding to the impression of 'dead frontage'. A post office and local hotel are key to generating footfall. The area started to decline soon after a Safeway store opened within a few hundred metres.

The Upperthorpe Community Alliance, which occupies a previously derelict shop, worked with the Council to secure necessary SRB funding for upgrading the area. In recognition of the shopping area's local social importance, the Alliance allocated funds (match-funded by the Council) to improve the environment and streetscape.

A common approach to shop frontage is a first step to promoting a collective identity for the area. The Alliance is also working with the Council on traffic calming and pedestrian safety. Plans include public art and better street lighting. Also of issue is the redesign of the back areas of the shops to curb anti-social uses such as drug dealing. The Alliance is in discussion with the Council on the management of public open space in the area and hopes to secure employment benefits for local residents in a service agreement.

In addition, local businesses can apply for grants for upgrading of premises from a private-sector-led initiative. A condition of grant is that investment should assist job creation or protect local jobs. Representation on the board of this initiative provides the Alliance with an opportunity to act as a first point of contact. This also provides a basis for dialogue between Alliance and local businesses on issues such as traffic management and business development.

The Alliance is also encouraging a range of alternative uses for vacant shop units, including the Sheffield Community Enterprise Development Unit, which provides business advice and support to community enterprises. Other units have been taken up by a recycling group and young people's project.

Points of inspiration

- *Key role for community alliance*: the local community plays a key role in reversing retail decline, working closely with the local council and other stakeholders, and with regeneration funding to hand.

- *Social investment a first step*: investment in a healthy living centre, community library and public baths provided a positive starting point for upgrading retail vitality. The regeneration strategy links retailing to community activity to build confidence in the area, to increase footfall and to take up vacant shop units by providing space for social organisations that help community development.

- *Practical retail strategy*: the need to balance community aspirations against what is commercially viable is important. The strategy identifies niche markets and encourages traders willing to take risks in

Business resource centre at the entrance to Upperthorpe high street. The offices of the Community Alliance are in a restored shop nearby.

A striking new medical centre with chemist is an attractive investment in Upperthorpe, providing social benefits and increasing footfall.

these areas. It is important to encourage complementary uses that promote footfall.

Constraints on regeneration

- *Need to secure 'social' planning gain*: local activists wish that planning authorities had been more proactive when Safeway was granted planning permission, to secure community benefits in terms of local employment. The Community Alliance also argues that its task would be easier if businesses in deprived areas were eligible for rates relief, as in enterprise zones.

FERNDALE, RHONDDA CYNON TAFF

A lively high street in a former mining town, surviving deindustrialisation, depopulation of the Valleys and arrival of superstores, aided by the restoration of a derelict chapel at its heart.

Key points

- Listed chapel, restored after legal battles by a local community development trust, now a social and educational centre, including cinema and training facilities.
- Future reinforcement of retail vitality will be undertaken by local partnership within the context of strategic renewal, and local shopkeepers and residents would like increased opportunity for real participation.

Synopsis

The high street is surviving even subsidised bus services to superstores. The chapel provides an attractive physical focus, but also a social centre which supports community spirit. This reinforces Ferndale as a destination and increases footfall. The restoration won a British Urban Regeneration Association national award.

Ferndale is a modest-sized town. Although unemployment is high, it has an attractive appearance and good quality of life, particularly now that strides have been made in reclamation of mining land, which has become green countryside.

Ferndale has a lively high street of more than 25 shops including: two butchers, two chemists, two supermarkets (Co-op and Spar), two banks, a baker, jeweller, travel agent, ironmonger, flowershop and others – in short, an array of shops which many towns would envy. There is also a new surgery and library. The narrow high street is the main route up the valley, busy with pedestrians and cars.

Ferndale has survived the arrival of a number of food superstores in Rhondda over the previous decade, some of which offer free or low-cost (10 or 20p) bus services to their premises. These retailer-subsidised services have carried as many as 250,000 passengers per year per store to the main towns and superstores. Funded from 'head office' to bolster custom, the budget is controlled by the local store manager who tailors the routes to suit local requirements.

Despite this option for their customers, most of Ferndale's retailers continue to trade profitably. One recent event that has helped maintain retail vitality was restoration of a derelict chapel standing at the main intersection, which made an enormous difference to the physical attractiveness of the town centre. The chapel, Trerhondda, was restored after much struggle by Ferndale's Community Development Trust (CDT), Arts Factory.[1] Abandoned by its congregation, which could not afford to repair its leaky roof, it was slated for demolition by the (now defunct) local borough council, which was petitioning for removal of listed building status. Approached by the Arts Factory, the council stuck to its stance, even resorting to veiled threats to force the CDT out of business. The Arts Factory on the other hand could see that the chapel was potentially a vital community asset. Demolition of the town's architectural heritage hardly seemed the way forward.

The Arts Factory collected 6,000 signatures from Valley residents and mounted a media campaign. The Secretary of State ordered a public inquiry with the decision going to restoration. Today, Trerhondda provides the town's social heart, replacing not only the demolished cinema but also lost working men's clubs. It has a mother and toddlers' group, youth outreach team, citizens' advice surgery and offers further education classes in a variety of subjects, such as computer training. It serves as an art exhibition area, houses a graphic design business and provides community meeting facilities. The congregation who could not afford its upkeep have now returned to worship there. The big screen cinema operates as a free film club. Craft fairs are held, which reinforces the town as a destination. Trerhondda takes care to support local retailing but not to compete. For example, there is no café, because there are local cafés nearby.

Other initiatives to support retailing are now emerging, in part because of the injection of Objective 1 monies, and because of the emerging community planning initiative, overseen by the local authority of Rhondda Cynon Taff (RCT). A previous scheme for shop-front renewal has evolved into a commercial improvement grant

Historic chapel saved from demolition and renovated by the local development trust provides a centre point to Ferndale's high street with community offices, meeting space, educational facilities and a full screen cinema club.

scheme, supporting premises improvement, business planning and e-commerce.

The newly evolving community planning initiative, with Wales Communities First regeneration funding stream, offers potential for linking top-down strategic planning for retailing and town centres with bottom-up local planning. RCT, for example, has established a strategic plan for town centre renewal, with a hierarchy of initiatives. Ferndale falls into the third phase, which links retail and social regeneration.

Points of inspiration

- *Local action through community development trust*: Trerhondda is a good example of organised community action through the development trust framework, nurturing a positive relationship between retail premises and social facilities to reinforce footfall while promoting social and economic development.

Constraints on regeneration

- *Need to reinforce retail vitality through local planning and investment*: shopkeepers in Ferndale would like to participate more actively to promote the town as a retail destination, and not just on an occasional basis. New mechanisms, such as through Community Planning, could provide this opportunity for participation over many years. Local shopkeepers would also like to see more investment in urban design: pavements, seating areas, public sculpture, flower planting and so on. They would also like to see investment in annual events, such as a carnival, which could reinforce the village in social and commercial terms.

- *Shop security grilles give forbidding evening appearance*: As in many retail areas, security grilles give a forbidding appearance out of hours, particularly those which allow no view of the shop's interior. Given that security and appearance can be achieved by better design of grilles, early attention to this both locally and in planning policy may be indicated.

GREEN STREET, LONDON BOROUGH OF NEWHAM

Enhancement of the retail and social vitality of a London high street and covered market.

Key points

- Creative strategy linking retailers and local council transformed a local shopping street into an Asian-specialty regional destination, while serving local needs.
- Refurbished high street environment with better balance between cars and pedestrians, and public art programme involving residents and schoolchildren.
- As in many partnerships, stakeholders' differing interests generate tension.

Synopsis

Building on the clustering of specialist ethnic retailers, the Green Street Partnership has acted in a creative way to enlarge its catchment, and to tie retail regeneration to social and educational objectives. The success is visible. Like many partnerships, problems of communication and tensions over investment decisions and issues such as parking need constant attention, but there is also 'creative tension' in the Council and retailers working together.

Green Street is a long high street, a stone's throw from the West Ham football ground. Newham is the most ethnically diverse London borough, with a majority of its population from minority ethnic households. Thirty years ago, Green Street was predominantly populated by Jewish traders, most of who achieved prosperity and departed to greener pastures. This indicates a key challenge to the Borough – to retain higher income households rather than merely be a 'staging post' on the road to prosperity.

Since the first Asian traders arrived in the 1960s, Green Street has become a significant destination for Asian clothing, jewellery and foodstuffs. There is also a covered market fronting Green Street, the Queens Market, on the site of an old street market. At busy times, there are more than 100 market stallholders trading alongside 20 permanent shops, which enclose the market on either side. The market structure has rooftop parking.

At the advent of SRB, Newham Council launched a first-round bid to:

- cement the retail vitality of Green Street and Queens Market, and reduce a 10 per cent shop vacancy rate by environmental improvements and by co-operative marketing efforts with retailers

- use the retail initiative to foster education and training, given minority ethnic unemployment 50 per cent higher than the area average

- support community and housing initiatives

- mount a community safety initiative.

The Green Street Partnership includes representatives from traders' associations, community and educational interests and local councillors. Total SRB investment in the area has been £8.1 m., rising to £17.6 m. with match funding. To achieve its ends, the Partnership works closely with Newham College, which has a business education and training centre in a historic, restored community education facility.

The centre, Barclay Hall, offers courses, crèche facilities, computer lab and a community meeting hall. It is especially concerned with the needs of women in the job market and residents wishing to start businesses.

The SRB initiative goes beyond retailing with expenditure on schools and community projects, women's programmes and housing improvements. The main expenditures in the retail sector have been: environmental improvements – particularly pavement widening – pedestrian crossings and creation of mosaic displays; improvements to the market including new canopies to mark its entrance; and a marketing campaign, described below. Other SRB investments have been made in local schools, particularly in IT and science labs, and in community projects.

At one point, the partnership almost came off the rails when traders felt that they had not been consulted over imposition of a controlled parking zone (CPZ). A meeting was hastily called but traders felt their views were still ignored and they took court action against the Council. Subsequently, the CPZ was instigated but with provision of off-street parking, with traders getting concessions. Some traders also resisted footway widening as detrimental, although evidence is for increased footfall and better turnover.

There is evidence that the retail programme is bearing fruit. Visitor surveys, carried out by students at Newham College, have documented a rise in visitors from outside the Borough from 15 per cent of shoppers to 34 per cent during the SRB. The intention by way of an exit strategy would be to put in place a town centre management regime, to address environment and cleansing, and to revitalise a retailer-managed marketing forum.

Points of inspiration

- *High quality environment*: widened pavements have enabled a vibrant shopping environment, while allowing a reasonable traffic flow. The balance has been shifted in favour of pedestrians without losing the linear high street feel. Of special interest is the use of SRB and council funding to link local primary schools, a secondary school and three community groups for elders with environmental artists to create a series of pavement mosaics on local themes, backed up by a community exhibition and poetry project.

- *Marketing strategy*: a unique initiative has been use of £140,000 of SRB funds spread over seven years to market Green Street as a regional destination, co-ordinated by a council officer with experience in media and visitor promotion. A first step was to hire, for a modest fee, consultants concerned with branding and image. They synthesised the Asian products on sale into four themes which defined the campaign – fashion materials, jewellery, clothing and foodstuffs – and identified a target audience of affluent, second-generation Asians. Key themes were expressed in a advertising campaign of posters on the sides of London buses, with a glossy photo for each theme and the strap line 'This is Green St'. Another ran 'Oxford St, Bond St, Green St'. Other campaigns included radio advertising, ads in regional Asian print media and a 30-second ad on an Asian-oriented

Wide pavements in Green Street give traders a chance to mount beautiful displays of food and shoppers room to browse. Footfall and turnover have increased.

Attention to environmental quality including new ornamental street lighting and, here, a road closed to create public space, makes Green Street an attractive destination.

satellite TV – reported to have been seen in Geneva! The modest promotion budget has been augmented in three ways. First, every ad campaign has included a local month-long promotion devised by the council officer and the retailers, such as a 'Hot Shopping Month' including storefront displays, gift giveaways, a customers' lottery and branded carrier bags. Second, every supplier of services has been encouraged to offer discounts to build a client base with local retailers. Third, retailers have moved into self-marketing, for example, commissioning glossy photo-ads in the *Vogue*-like magazine, *Asian Woman*.

Constraints on regeneration

- *Parking*: provision remains an issue, especially as Green Street cements its objective of becoming a regional destination – many shoppers arrive by car. Although additional off-street space has been provided, in part by the use by the Council of compulsory purchase powers, and the CPZ controls on-street parking, residents naturally feel there is too much traffic, while traders feel there is not enough customer parking.

- *The future of Queens Market*: as of this writing, Queens Market traders are concerned that council interests see spiralling London property prices as an opportunity to demolish a poorly designed, expensive-to-maintain market hall, and free up a site for redevelopment. One aspect of concern is that the Council, as their landlord, can avoid renewing leases thereby undercutting the traders' association's membership base. Few stallholders have the financial wherewithal to suffer any protected period of uncertainty.

Existing market hall

BOROUGH MARKET, LONDON BOROUGH OF SOUTHWARK
Regeneration of a historic inner London market dating from 1756.

Key points
- A market run by a community-based development trust offers an organisational model for other off-street markets.
- Marketing strategy based on augmenting retail function for high quality farm and organic produce, intended to serve local residents and a wider catchment, and refurbishment of local shops for food-related businesses.

Synopsis
Contraction of the market's wholesale function necessitated an expansion of its role back into retailing, as it was more than one hundred years ago. Its trustees have developed a regeneration and marketing strategy based on high quality retail provision, food-related training and business development, and refurbishment of local shops.

The first record of Borough Market is in 1014 AD. It was established at its present 4.5 acre site by an Act of Parliament in 1756. It was a retail market selling a wide variety of food until the late nineteenth century when it became a wholesale market trading from the ringing of a bell at 9.00 p.m. through the night. The market consists of a glass-roofed structure, with two Victorian railway viaducts running over its top, and offices facing Borough High Street. The market is administered by a non-profit development trust, managed by 21 trustees who live locally and are nominated by community groups. The market has a small staff including a market inspector, small business adviser, four beadles and two porters. The market's development trust status ensures that it works directly in the combined interests of local residents and for the healthy continuation of the market in perpetuity.

In recent years, the market's wholesale function has contracted, due to the centralised buying practices of major supermarket chains and to traffic congestion, which has caused all other wholesale markets to move from central to peripheral locations. Recent disturbance due to construction of the Jubilee Line has also created problems, and the market is now fighting proposals to widen the railway viaducts that cross it. The number of wholesalers has declined from around 150 in the market's heyday to 20 in 1994 and just nine today.

To meet these challenges and to assist in the regeneration of this inner city neighbourhood, the market has joined forces to establish a Borough Markets Partnership which brings it together with the Peabody Trust, the local council, churches, the residents' forum, nearby businesses and the market traders' association. Four years ago, with SRB funding, the Partnership embarked on a regeneration strategy. For the market itself, the key plank in the strategy is to position the market back to its earlier role as a retail market, but one based on high quality farm and organic produce. As part of this programme, the partnership has renovated its surrounding properties and filled them with new food-related tenants, started a retail market two days a week and established new food retailers within the market on a permanent basis.

It has buttressed this with an innovative marketing programme. This began with a weekend 'Food Lovers' Fair', with demonstrations by professional chefs, which was a great success and attracted television coverage. The retail market then opened one day a month, then Friday and Saturday once a month, now Friday and Saturday every week.

There is an annual three-day 'Apple Festival', organised in association with the charity Common Ground which celebrates rare and traditional varieties of British apples. This includes theatre performances in the market by a group that marches from the nearby Globe Theatre. The Apple Festival in turn is part of the Southwark Festival. The product range in the market now extends to fish, shrimp, scallops, game and poultry, wild mushrooms, organic beer and many other premium products. A 'London's larder' website ties together all the information on the market.

The partnership has embarked on a food-related training programme and a market trader programme led by the market, which also offers a small business advisory service and a childcare programme for local residents. A course leading to a Basic Food Hygiene Certificate is available for local restaurant staff.

Despite its marketing success, the market and the surrounding area still face challenges. The market structure is in poor shape and requires renovation. It is putting in place a regeneration package that combines market and public funds. Surrounding local shops have also been steadily renovated and let to food-related tenants. The market also has major improvement plans and has purchased the glass-house façade of Covent Garden's Floral Hall, which it now has in storage. It is intending to use this as a striking entrance to a new development of retail premises and as a significant urban design focus for the surrounding neighbourhood.

Points of inspiration
- *Repositioning with a view of strengths and market*: the market's repositioning has

recognised the enormous potential of a 'niche' which stresses high quality farm and organic produce. This enables it to serve local needs for better food and build a wider catchment in a sector of the marketplace where they do not come head to head with the big multiples and which is entirely suited to the premises.

- *Marketing strategy*: a strategy based on steadily attracting both additional customers and additional traders, the latter with on-site training available to them. Use of fairs and linkage to local Southwark fair gives visibility and indicates local commitment.

Borough Market, managed by a community trust since 1756, revitalises itself with an added role in high quality and organic food and keen marketing.

A new stallholder in Borough Market with an inviting display of artisan cheeses.

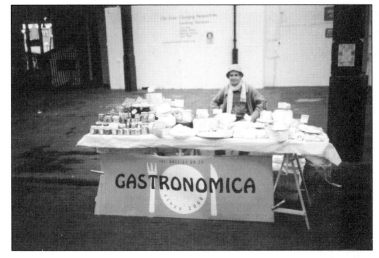

5 Starting over – new shopping areas within integrated regeneration initiatives

New local high street

CROWN STREET, GORBALS, GLASGOW

Re-creation of traditional urban streetscape including new shops and supermarket, most at street level under new residential tenements, on a 40-acre site.

Key points
- Master planning process, which has developed a new, but traditionally patterned, inner city tenemental neighbourhood out of a brownfield site.
- New shops and homes reflect commitment to quality urban design and traditional materials.
- Typical problems of anti-social behaviour need active management.
- Nearby developments could undermine retail regeneration.

Synopsis
The shopping street of the new neighbourhood is located just off a main route through the area to combine local and passing trade. Integration of new housing with shopping is readily apparent with a dozen retail businesses trading satisfactorily and with population set to grow as housing is occupied. Problems of shopper and store staff insecurity, and shoplifting, associated with a methadone maintenance programme are being addressed.

Infamous for having 100,000 people packed into a square mile of teeming nineteenth-century tenements, themselves built over earlier slums, the Gorbals underwent comprehensive renewal in the 1960s. Traditional stone tenements on a grid were replaced by system-built, multi-storey housing. With this demolition, 387 shops and 39 public houses disappeared, replaced by a shopping precinct at the base of a huge block of flats. Also disappearing were 'backcourts' crammed with small industries.

By the 1980s, what had been regarded as an architectural showpiece was in decline. A focus of resident disapproval was the notorious 'Hutchesontown E' blocks. Their demolition in 1989 left a site which was to be reborn as Crown Street. Central to regeneration was a vision of:

… an attractive and popular inner-city area served by a full range of local shops, public services and community facilities.

Crown Street is an important catalyst to regeneration of the Gorbals. The Gorbals Initiative is a partnership of the Glasgow Development Agency, Glasgow District Council and Scottish Homes. As a first step, master planning was initiated involving consultants and public participation, overseen by the active management of Crown Street Regeneration. Although there was initial consideration of redevelopment of the 1960s' shopping arcade, a number of factors influenced the decision to fashion an entirely new shopping environment:

- Crown Street's significance as a 'flagship' project for the Gorbals

- urban design objectives which intended to recreate an urban grid pattern

- the need to provide a quality shopping environment alongside new housing to attract new householders and create a mixed-tenure, mixed-income community.

The old shopping centre is soon to be demolished to make space for residential development and the new shopping area is nearly complete. There are currently 11 retail businesses operating, plus a new supermarket.

Crown Street Regeneration is committed to local economic development, to generate employment and contribute to retail vitality. For example, 11 railway arches have been refurbished as affordable locations for a variety of businesses. A new hotel has recently opened. However, a related phase of development, incorporating a pub, library, new church and additional business units, has been delayed due to difficulties in pulling together a funding package.

Points of inspiration

- *Master planning*: given principles of sustainability, and reintroduction of the traditional street pattern, new retail units fronting the street were a key objective. The decision to create a mixture of retail tenures is also intended to contribute to viability. Some shops were sold freehold; a property company bought two for onward letting and the rest are available on a commercial letting basis. Overall, the density of housing supports retail viability while the availability of adjacent shopping contributes to the marketability of new housing and quality of life in this new, but traditional, neighbourhood.

- *Quality urban design*: the incorporation of retail units into the traditional tenement form reflects a commitment to urban design. With shop design by the same architects responsible for housing, retailing is well integrated, fulfilling the intention of creating urban, rather than suburban, form. The standard of exterior finish, including use of natural sandstone which defines significant Glasgow

New townscape and shopping street at Crown Street in Glasgow's traditional tenemental form. The spacious pavement in the foreground fronts the new Kwik Save.

buildings, is superior to that normally achieved on commercial developments outside of established town centres.

Constraints on regeneration

- *Partnership*: there is concern that redevelopment of the area has proceeded at a slower pace than expected which has had a knock-on effect on retail vitality in the short term. As in any cleared regeneration area with phases of demolition and new build of housing, the numbers of households within the catchment area will decline before they begin to rise.

- *Security*: an unintended by-product of the provision of a chemist's in the retail mix has been public safety issues associated with a methadone maintenance

programme, including problems of shoplifting and mugging. Some commentators suggest profit is being put before community safety, and this situation was in danger of undermining investment in regeneration and the objective of creating a mixed-income neighbourhood. The issue is currently being addressed.

- *Threats to viability*: nearby development sites have received planning permission for a retail warehouse park, the latter including fast food and petrol station shop. These fit poorly with the vision of the master plan for a traditionally patterned, urban neighbourhood and may affect the viability of Crown Street.

New shopping centres

PENNYWELL, SUNDERLAND

New shopping centre which replaces a derelict 1960s' precinct at the heart of what used to be Sunderland's most stigmatised estate. A successful development with near full occupancy and an extended catchment.

Key points
- New-build centre is attractive to local residents and shoppers from further afield travelling by car and bus.
- Twenty-four hour security and twice-a-day cleaning maintain environmental quality and deter anti-social behaviour.
- Shopping centre linked to a new, popular community and health resource centre, which has attracted the estate's first resident health and primary care service.
- 'L'-shaped shopping centre gives high security but offers little urban design benefit.

Synopsis
Development around a car park anchored by a Kwik Save and Iceland, and with 11 units trading actively. The new-build approach was seen as essential to overcoming the poor reputation of the previous precinct and to broadening the catchment. A disadvantage is a car park as a focal point and the high security 'backside' of the 'L', which presents a monolithic, unwelcoming aspect to two sides of the surrounding neighbourhood.

In 1996, the City of Sunderland Partnership agreed that the Pennywell Estate and surrounding area, home to 9,500 residents, should be top priority for regeneration. At this time, 78 per cent of younger residents wanted to leave the area as soon as possible. Among aspects of Pennywell's poor reputation, it was known as the 'car crime capital of Europe' and the sink estate of Sunderland.

Even before this, however, the recognised challenge facing the local development organisation, the Pride in Pennywell campaign – later the SRB-funded Proving Partnership Works (PPW) – was to restore pride in the area and to give local people a central role in developing a positive future for the estate. Pride in Pennywell linked local residents with business and political leaders at the city level. A multi-dimensional economic and social programme was developed. This included attention to the run-down shopping precinct on Pennywell Green at the estate's heart.

At one time, the precinct had been prosperous, anchored by a Woolworth's and with many active shops. But decline set in during the 1980s, exacerbated by fire damage. By 1990, only two shops and two takeaways were trading, the upper floors had become derelict and drunkenness and glue sniffing were widespread. Around the same time, the property company that owned the centre went out of business, creating a management hiatus.

A crucial decision was taken not to renovate the existing centre, but to demolish it and build a new shopping centre across the road on open space. The intentions were to:

- create a new image of the shopping centre and not to attempt to build on the old, stigmatised image

- create an investment opportunity for a private developer-manager

- make the centre relevant to local needs

- increase its viability by making it attractive to car-borne shoppers, and by attracting anchor tenants appropriate to the market

- make it secure by design, CCTV, round-the-clock security, and by night-time functions such as takeaway and video rental shops

- make the centre a social as well as retail destination by development of a community, health and medical resource centre.

Although there were some objections to the take-up of green space, and concern of the few remaining retailers over future rents, Pride in Pennywell persisted with its new-build programme, to great success. The Pennywell Shopping Centre, owned and managed by a private company in association with Kwik Save and Iceland, opened in 1995. The land that the centre sits on was 'donated' to the development consortium by the Council as a means of promoting inward investment.

The centre is now trading successfully, with almost every unit rented. Tenants include fruit and vegetable shop, food takeaway, chemist, post office, betting shop, newsagent, baker and a mini-cab office. There is also a police outpost, used mainly as a 'surgery', and the office of PPW. Across the road, the previous site now contains an attractive sheltered housing development.

Points of inspiration

- *Extended catchment*: the relocation/new-build decision, attraction of anchor food store tenants, a range of shops and services such as mini-cab and visible, secure parking area all benefit local residents but also attract shoppers from further afield, contributing to retail viability.

- *Security and cleanliness*: a 24-hour-per-day, seven-days-per-week security guard and monitoring CCTV are seen as essential. 'Hanging out' is discouraged and there is little vandalism. Sunderland Council has provided a dedicated cleaning regime, which was extended from once to twice a day as soon as it was apparent that a single daily clean was insufficient.

- *Attached community centre*: the new Pennywell Neighbourhood and Medical Centre, opened in 2000, owned by a locally managed, non-profit trust. This brings a further flow of residents into the shopping centre. The site is leased from the Council on a 99-year lease. Prior to its opening, the estate had no GP or childcare facilities. These are now provided, with a Primary Care Team supplemented by an antenatal and mum and baby clinic, parent and toddler facility, teenage health information service, a course in 'Parenting Power' and a 'Young at Heart' group for elderly residents. The community centre, in partnership with other agencies, also provides childcare training for local residents and a school holiday activity programme attended by more than 1,300 young people. The centre is open until 9.00 p.m., which contributes to the area's liveliness in the evening.

Points of concern

- *Quality of urban design*: the catchment has been extended by making the centre attractive to car-based shoppers. This is important because Pennywell still suffers from a high void rate in social housing and the numbers of local residents are insufficient to support a full range of shops. The attractiveness of the centre is

The new shopping centre at Pennywell has helped turn around perceptions of a stigmatised estate and provides a valuable retail resource for local residents.

in part due to the range of shops, but also to the typical 'L'-shaped design, which enfolds a car park with two arms of shops and makes it constantly visible. This type of design, much the same as in Seacroft, Leeds and other locations, works well for car park security, but raises concerns over its urban design quality in that the backsides of the development, not facing the car park, are basically a solid wall, impenetrable to the public and unattractive.

SEACROFT GREEN, LEEDS

Demolition and rebuilding of a district shopping centre in East Leeds to give a 110,000 sq. ft Tesco Extra and ten additional shops.

Key points

- Rebuild intended to side-step the area's poor reputation and turn a declining local centre into a sub-regional destination.
- Challenge by Leeds City Council, and commitment by Tesco, to create 300 jobs for unemployed local residents in return for planning permission. First of a series of initiatives by which Tesco intends to create 2,000 jobs in regeneration areas.
- New bus station promotes public transport use.
- 'L'-shaped design presents a forbidding 'backside' to the community.

Synopsis

The declining 1960s' shopping centre was plagued by crime and anti-social behaviour. The Council opted for demolition and Tesco made a commitment to job creation through a Seacroft Partnership. The new centre is 100 per cent occupied. It includes good bus links through a new bus station adjacent to the Tesco store, although the centre's car-park-oriented design tends to turn its back on the community.

Seacroft Green's redevelopment involved the complete rebuilding of a new-town-style district shopping centre and market hall serving a number of estates at the periphery of Leeds. It is the first of a series of partnership initiatives between Tesco, the New Deal for Employment and local stakeholders to invest in brownfield sites, and to link food retailing to training and employment creation. The Seacroft Partnership includes Leeds City Council, Tesco, developers Asda St James, Employment Service, the East Leeds Family Learning Centre and shopworkers' union USDAW.

Seacroft Green was fully let through the 1980s, but the centre was never profitable for the Council and its popularity was on the wane. By 1990, it was in decline, in part due to anti-social behaviour. Shoppers suffered car crime and there were burnt-out wrecks littering the area. The centre was difficult to police due to an underground parking garage and 'nooks and crannies' in the original design. The whole area suffered from stigma, which caused all of the multiple retailers and its six banks to move elsewhere. There were also structural problems due to concrete failure, with the fire marshal threatening closure.

Following an option study by consultants, in 1995, a decision for demolition was taken by the Council, which owned the centre. The consultant's conclusion was that, given its location on the ring road, the site had retail potential but the existing physical fabric and centre's reputation did not support that aspiration. Demolition was intended to address the stigma of the old centre in one go. Compulsory purchase orders were used to shift a few tenants with long ground leases. Other tenants were promised space in the redevelopment and one parade of shops was left standing during demolition to provide for local requirements.

During this period, the Council had many discussions with potential retail investors. The Council's aspiration was for a moderate-size food unit of about 50,000 sq. ft as an anchor for a new shopping centre. But existing local provision of moderate-size supermarkets within a few miles, and tight profitability in this size range, meant there was no retailer interest in a mid-size store. Following consultations, Tesco approached the Council and argued that a large-format store, with a sub-regional catchment, would be viable, given economies of scale and the low land value of the site in a deprived area.

The new development opened in 2000. It is a modern, attractive centre, typically 'L'-shaped with shops facing the car park. It is anchored by a 'Tesco Extra' whose product range includes not only food, but also clothing, electrical goods, mobile phones and toys. There is also a post office, bank, travel agent, baker and five other shops. In the car park, there is a bus station with frequent local and regional services to many destinations. The Council retains the freehold but takes no income at this stage. There are, however, 'profit claw back' arrangements in place.

A particular thrust of the development is to secure employment benefits. To this end, Tesco entered into agreement with the East Leeds Family Learning Centre, to organise training and childcare. Applicants are selected by the Employment Service and sent to college to learn basic working skills. The Partnership's employment strategy states that, in the first instance, 240 of the 320 new workers at the store will be former long-term unemployed local residents. This goal has been exceeded.

In association with the redevelopment, a nearby local health centre is being refurbished. Although there are no social facilities associated with this phase of the development, there is potential in future to revitalise a local bingo hall and a listed school building for community facilities.

Points of inspiration
- *Local employment and retail benefits*: Tesco has made good on its promise to Leeds City Council to create a substantial number of jobs for local unemployed persons. In part, this has been enabled by Tesco's commitment to working through local training and further education organisations. On the retail side, local residents now have access to a substantial range of goods at reasonable prices, without needing a car to do so.

- *Private sector lead in partnership*: although a member of the partnership, Leeds City Council allowed Tesco and the training sector to lead on the all-important training initiative. Consensus is that the private sector has been able to move much faster than the public sector in this area, enabling the partnership to achieve its objectives efficiently.

Constraints on regeneration

- *Lack of retention of local traders*: as in other locations such as Hulme, complete demolition of an operating retail centre dealt directly and positively with a poor reputation. But it also disrupted the existing retail base and meant loss of existing retail presence. Also as elsewhere, in the absence of monitoring during redevelopment, it is difficult to assess the impact. Some traders relocated; others retired or went out of business. Some, trading at the margin, may have gone out of business in any event. Assurances were given to Seacroft Green's independent traders that disruption would be minimised and there was discussion about a new market hall for local stallholders, but this never materialised. In the end, not one trader

Tesco at Seacroft Green provides significant local employment benefits, and broadens the range of food and goods available locally. Although there is a good bus station on site, many shoppers arrive by car – an environmental issue that needs to be addressed at national and regional levels.

The rear elevation of 'L'-shaped shopping centres like Seacroft Green are good for security but can present a forbidding aspect to the local neighbourhood and deter easy access by pedestrians.

from the previous centre found a place in the new development, which consists almost entirely of multiple retailers.

- *Urban design*: as at Sunderland, Seacroft's 'L'-shaped design consists of a structure enclosing a car park. In the words of one resident, 'It's no longer a town centre, just a shopping centre'. For security and servicing reasons, it bluntly turns its back on the surrounding community, with no point of entry from anywhere but the car park. In terms of site, the centre's hilltop position means that the back side of the development stands over the existing community with an appearance reminiscent of a prison. On the shop side where the old centre, for all its faults, provided social space, there is only space for parking, purchasing and waiting for the bus.

New shopping centre plus new high street

HULME HIGH STREET, MANCHESTER

Redevelopment of a 1960s' shopping precinct, giving a new food superstore and two attached retail units, which anchor the development of a new high street, market hall and community centre.

Key points

- A phased development, intended to attract new investment to a stigmatised area with a poor reputation, by creating the opportunity for a large food store adjacent to a busy highway.
- Using this as an anchor for new high street and market hall.
- Loss of existing retail presence.

Synopsis

Comprehensive redevelopment included strong commitment to retail regeneration in two phases. The first saw construction of a food superstore. The logic is that through traffic accesses the superstore, widening its catchment, without needing to drive into Hulme itself. Under construction is the new high street which bridges Hulme and Moss Side. The new market hall is now open.

Hulme, once a dense neighbourhood of two-storey houses clustered around a bustling high street, was cleared and redeveloped in the 1960s. The local high street, Stretford Road, was replaced by a shopping precinct and market hall in a different location.

The redeveloped area deteriorated, with Hulme's reputation declining with it. In a second round of redevelopment over the last decade, Hulme has been completely rebuilt again. Regeneration is based on a hierarchy of traditional streets, 'human in scale but urban in nature' (Hulme Regeneration Ltd, 1994). At the heart of regeneration are more than 2,000 new flats and houses. A strong housing market is seen as important in establishing the area's credibility. Hulme Regeneration Ltd (HRL), a partnership of City Council and AMEC plc with

- new 'high street' with a mix of retail and service uses

- neighbourhood shopping in Stretford Road

- local facilities at three other locations

- individual corner shops.

The main thrust of this was that re-creation of a new high street in Stretford Road was commercially difficult, and that a more viable option was to create a high street adjacent to a new food superstore next to a main highway. This would give passing motorists a close look at the changed Hulme's new shopping facilities and attract car-borne trade, which would benefit local residents by providing a wide range of goods. The redeveloped area, with parking for 650 cars, is called 'Hulme High Street', a joint venture between AMEC plc and Manchester City Council.

The redevelopment of the 30-acre shopping area was put to tender and won by an AMEC subsidiary. The high street portion of the development (to be completed in 2002) is expected to provide a social focus for the area and includes an indoor and outdoor market (totalling 35,000 sq. ft) and a range of retail and commercial facilities. With the design and developer in place, no financial incentives were necessary in attracting supermarket interest, with Asda persuaded on the quality of the location. Asda opened its 86,000 sq. ft store in 1998 with two warehouse units, currently occupied by a catalogue company and a discount outlet. The food store was financed and built to Asda's specifications.

The new market has been developed by a partnership between AMEC and French market

At a community planning event, residents had agreed with proposals for the old centre's demolition. There was consensus for a new high street. However, community representatives also highlighted the need for continuity for local traders throughout redevelopment. The community's proposal was to replace the enclosed centre with an open thoroughfare, with Stretford Road reinstated as a high street. Redevelopment was to build on the positive aspects of the old precinct including the 60 shop and stallholders, the latter in particular known for Afro-Caribbean food and products. However, the centre and market hall were closed long in advance of replacement facilities and this led to around two-thirds of local traders closing shop with many of the rest moving to Moss Side.

In 1993, as a result of market analysis, HRL proposed a hierarchy of shopping:

operators Groupe Geraud, which runs 300 municipal markets across Europe. The market provides internal food stalls and a new public square with scope for additional outdoor stalls. The partnership intends to build upon the Afro-Caribbean character of the area to promote the market hall as a catalyst to footfall. However, given that many past traders have moved to other areas, promotion of the market hall is a key challenge. It is hoped that some market traders, once established, may trade up to retail units on the High Street.

There is every indication that many local residents find the Asda a welcome addition to Hulme in terms of the variety of goods on offer, prices and local employment benefits. The latter have proved a striking success with over 80 per cent of the 400 Asda employees previously unemployed and, of those, 51 per cent of a minority ethnic origin. It was also felt that the store has provided a new meeting place for residents. However, residents are also aware of the superstore's negative impacts, such as its role in undermining local shops and its high degree of dependence on car-borne shoppers. There are also concerns that Asda has cut into the local ethnic retail market as it logically diversifies its product range to cater for minority ethnic tastes.

Points of inspiration

- *Master plan*: the decision to package sites with clear design briefs within the context of an overall master plan was critical to success. This enables developers to tailor facilities to market demand. Emphasis on commercial considerations in design is said to bolster investor confidence.

- *Joint venture company*: transfer of redevelopment responsibility from the formal decision-making process of Manchester City Council to a joint venture company with strong development experience allowed retail regeneration to be driven forward outside of the slower time frame of council decision making. At the same time, the Council is part of the joint venture board with an important stake in the project.

- *Training and recruitment*: the key to Asda's effectiveness in local recruitment was in working with experienced local organisations, such as Moss Side and Hulme Community Development Trust. This built upon the good relationship these organisations had with local people.

- *Phasing and investor confidence*: throughout the development, AMEC took a commercial decision not to flood the market with an oversupply of retail accommodation. It was felt that too many vacant units would create a poor impression and could undermine emerging investor confidence in Hulme. Careful phasing of development helped build success.

Constraints on regeneration

- *Lack of support for existing businesses*: the need for early demolition diverted attention from the need to support existing businesses during redevelopment. Failure to put new facilities in place meant that displaced businesses had nowhere to go. Although market traders were moved to temporary accommodation in a vacant local pub, this proved inadequate, with the premises subsequently closed on environmental

The new market hall under construction at Hulme High Street and now open.

The layout of Hulme High Street with the mall car park visible and accessible from a main highway, and the new high street linking Hulme and Moss Side.

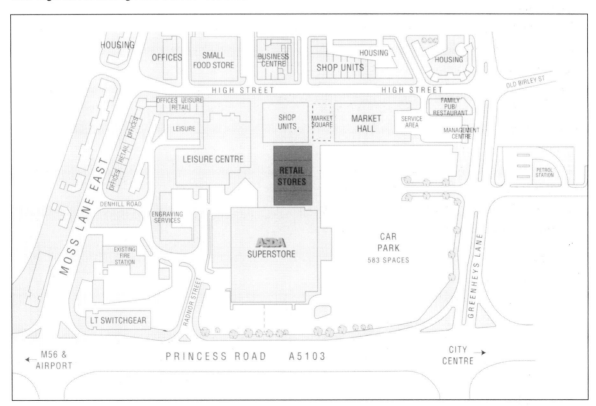

health grounds. Redevelopment had a particularly negative impact on marginal businesses, many of which folded.

- *Car dependence and the quality of urban design*: like many new developments in regeneration areas, a priority has been to attract retail investment and to widen the potential catchment of the businesses to be established. This has meant opting for the currently popular shopping mall premises, highly dependent on car-borne shoppers. Although the decision makes commercial sense, little attention is paid to social costs in terms of air pollution from cars. Like most such developments, it is also pedestrian-unfriendly, and low in design quality, being mainly facing a large car park with wide access roads. This type of development runs counter to the urban aspirations set out in Hulme's design guide. It remains to be seen if the new high street will temper this lack of urban design quality.

6 The lessons of a regional shopping centre

A major regional centre on a brownfield site

BRAEHEAD RETAIL CENTRE, RENFREWSHIRE

A massive retail and leisure complex in Scotland, on 285 acres and with parking for 6,500 vehicles, located on derelict land near, but not close enough to walk to, the Scottish Social Inclusion Partnership areas in Govan and Paisley.

Key points
- Multi-use development, encompassing retailing, leisure, housing and public parkland, regenerating 285 acres of derelict land in a former shipbuilding area along the Clyde.
- Reasonable, if not entirely successful, attempt to secure local employment benefits through partnership.
- Shopping centre developer-management company has joined Paisley Town Centre Vision Partnership.
- Almost completely car-dependent with little attention to environmental implications or effect on neighbouring town centres.

Synopsis

Phase 1 has included 100+ stores. A modest number of jobs for nearby residents have been secured, although most have gone to residents of the wider region. Problems in training of residents included slow start by public agencies, lack of experience of large retail projects, insufficient co-ordination of public agencies and poor information flows between training agencies and retailers. No assessment of the implications for CO_2 emissions or other environmental factors, although some traffic-impact forecasting was undertaken.

Braehead, which opened in 1999, is promoted as the focal point of a major regeneration initiative for Clyde-side brownfield land within the Glasgow–Paisley conurbation. The centre's M8 location makes it accessible to around 50 per cent of Scotland's population within a 45-minute drive. The site was previously derelict, close to two Social Inclusion Partnership (SIP) areas: Paisley Partnership and the Govan Initiative. Braehead is one of the biggest out-of-town retail centres approved in Scotland, and thus a different order of case study. Planning permission for the development predated the 1998 revision of Scotland's national planning guidance on shopping (NPPG 8), so it was not required to respond to a 'sequential' test.

Proposals for Braehead provoked controversy. The former Strathclyde Regional Council refused planning permission and both Glasgow City and Renfrewshire Councils objected. The Councils' objection was that the centre would undermine structure plan policy of sustaining and improving existing shopping centres by directing investment to them, and would have adverse impact on existing retail viability. Following a public inquiry, consent for the scheme was granted by the then Secretary of State on appeal in June 1990.

Although not recognised as appropriate within the former Structure Plan, Braehead figures prominently within the latest Plan as a 'gateway' to promote the growth in the Clyde corridor. A mixed-use second phase, including housing, is planned. The associated redevelopment of the riverside walkway, provision of a maritime heritage centre and construction of nine light industrial units in Govan were secured as planning gain.

The extent of the development

The site is owned and managed by Capital Shopping Centres Ltd (CSC) whose portfolio includes the Lakeside and Metro Centres. It was developed in association with Marks & Spencer and J. Sainsbury. The development was undertaken as a straightforward commercial exercise and received no public subsidy. Public involvement was confined mainly to attempting to secure for local residents training and employment opportunities from the development.

Phase 1, covering 110 acres and costing £285 m., is largely complete and includes:

- shopping mall
- retail warehouse park
- 4,000-seat, multi-purpose arena
- ice complex
- maritime heritage centre
- bus station, coach park, taxi rank, 600 cycle spaces, cycle routes
- business park.

The shopping mall is anchored by Marks & Spencer's and a Sainsbury's Savacentre. Sixteen million customers visited the centre during the first 12 months. Outside the centre, but adjacent, outline planning application is being submitted shortly for Phase 2 to include new homes, hotel, parkland and further entertainment outlets.

Aspects relevant to social inclusion

As a site derelict for 20 years, Braehead represented a major opportunity for employment generation and was intended to contribute to employment opportunity for residents in the adjacent SIPs. Estimates of jobs created vary. According to CSC, building work offered 3,500 jobs rising to 5,000 just before the centre opened, but other sources suggest 2,500 construction jobs at peak (Glass and McGregor, 2000). Although opportunities for promoting employment in construction tended to be limited due to use of subcontractors, it was written into contracts that, in those cases where a contractor did not utilise existing staff, the Employment Service would fill those positions.

Once the shopping centre opened, around 3,000 jobs became available, 600 of which were to be filled through an on-site recruitment centre, with the remainder filled by internal transfers and individual store advertising. A recent analysis provides a critical assessment of job take-up (Glass and McGregor, 2000). Of all jobs, approximately two-thirds were filled by women and one-third by men. Around a fifth of posts created were filled by internal transfers from stores elsewhere and the majority by direct selection by the stores themselves. The researchers concluded that the part-time nature of work available and low hourly rates limited the social inclusion impacts to be achieved within the nearby regeneration areas, with some residents on benefit not finding the take-home pay sufficient to warrant leaving the benefit system. However, 97 per cent of jobs were filled by Renfrewshire residents and those from the wider Glasgow area. Significantly, the survey found that only 2 per cent of jobs were taken up by the long-term unemployed, defined as out of work for six months or more. The researchers describe the figure for the long-term unemployed recruitment as 'very disappointing'. However, it was felt that intense pressure on retailers to open on time tended to work against the development of inclusive employment and training programmes. As one respondent put it, 'when there is an urgency to the task, the inclusiveness agenda goes out the window.'

Issues related to local retailing and transport
The general perception is that Braehead has impacted on the viability of nearby Paisley town centre, mainly at the margins. While the amount of vacant floor space in the town centre rose slightly around the time of Braehead's opening to 13.7 per cent of the total (from 12.14 per cent in 1996), more recently this has declined to 10.3 per cent (Renfrewshire Council, unpublished). However, there has been leakage of spending from higher social groups from the town centre, reflected in the current tenant mix. The centre has impacted negatively on smaller, independent stores rather than on national retailers. However, Paisley has also suffered from competition from retail expansion in neighbouring local authority areas and growing customer expectations, perhaps better served by a climate-controlled shopping centre. For their part, CSC claims that the centre was never intended to 'steal trade' and that the key objective is to promote the West of Scotland as a major retail destination.

A positive development has been initiation of a Paisley Town Centre Vision Partnership, of which CSC is a member. The Partnership has sub-groups on retail promotion, the public realm, marketing and a range of initiatives to develop Paisley's distinctiveness as a niche centre utilising existing resources such as its architectural historical heritage and its university.

In transport terms, the development was not subject to a traffic impact assessment, although a proposed neighbouring Ikea development will be. Although there have been vague proposals to integrate the development with water taxis linked to Glasgow's underground, to provide a ferry service linking it across the river to Glasgow's West End and to re-establish rail connections, the centre's dependence on car-borne shoppers is established. In terms of private funding for non-car transport, the costs of implementing other options is now unlikely to yield an increase in retail and leisure trade sufficient to justify investment. Braehead is typical of British out-of-town shopping developments in that the great majority of its shoppers arrive by car, as was intended. No analysis has been undertaken on the implications for CO_2 emissions.

Points of inspiration
- *Proactive developer*: CSC put a local management team in place to create the necessary partnerships and links for job creation. Representatives contacted over 600 local business and community groups to alert them to potential opportunities. The developer also worked with public agencies in the recruitment stages, has now joined the Paisley Town Centre Vision Partnership and is co-operating

with Renfrewshire Council in area planning.

- *Mixed-use development*: regeneration benefits to be achieved were material to the Secretary of State's decision to approve the scheme, relating to the potential for shopping centres to act as a catalyst for other investments. This also coincides with retail trends in that the leisure component was to be integrated into the shopping centre to give a 'total leisure visit'. As plans for Phase 2 unfold, a long-standing derelict area could be transformed into a vibrant mixed-use area.

Constraints on regeneration

- *Low take-up of employment training*: both Paisley and Govan regeneration partnerships adopted an approach which tailored training to clients' needs, with training delivered through local colleges. Courses ranged from part-time to in-depth training including work placement. However, the numbers that went through training were disappointing. Of around 10,000 persons who registered an interest, 280 applicants undertook training. Explanations for low take-up included insufficient lead-time of agencies promoting training relative to the pace of development, delay between client registration and follow-up, and insufficient co-ordination between agencies. More positively, many residents who underwent training were successful in gaining employment. In Govan, 61 per cent gained some type of employment.

- *Lack of a common agenda for employment and training*: one area of frustration was over

an inability to set up courses fast enough at local colleges to enable stores to open with 'job-ready' staff. One reason for delay was that agencies involved came to the table with different agendas and at differing paces. The majority of locally based public sector partners were interested in creating opportunities for local residents and the long-term unemployed. This did not necessarily involve getting residents jobs but was about providing support to enable them to compete effectively in the job market. However, for the Employment Service, the key objective was in getting people into work whatever their home address. Based on the Employment Service's objective that all retail outlets would open with sufficient staff, the initiative was successful. This mismatch in organisational objectives carried through into employment monitoring which has made it difficult to assess local, as opposed to sub-regional, employment benefits. Hindsight suggests that greater co-ordination from the outset could have resolved this difficulty.

- *Time lag to public response*: because the project straddled administrative boundaries, two local enterprise companies were responsible for organising training through the local colleges. However, they did not respond to this challenge at the same pace and, in one case, courses were not organised until some time after recruitment began. As such, those responsible for training programmes felt they did not have enough time to make appropriate arrangements. Training programmes tended to be 'too little, too late'.

- *Poor links between training providers and employers*: training courses were intended to be relevant to employers' requirements. However, lack of feedback from employers regarding their initial requirements and the relative qualifications of successful and unsuccessful applicants meant that training agencies felt unable to gauge the effectiveness of programmes, or whether less vocational aspects were significant, such as interpersonal skills. Access to meaningful information could have enabled agencies to tailor programmes more effectively.

- *Addressing long-term unemployment*: a broad concern was whether short-term programmes are sufficient to prepare long-term unemployed residents of chronically deprived areas to compete in the job market – even for jobs nearby. A quick approach, as dictated by the need here to respond to market opportunities, may underestimate the deep-rooted nature of intergenerational unemployment and complex issues around self-esteem, self-confidence and personal development. Recognition of these issues has led the Enterprise Companies in the vicinity of Braehead to reconsider future project planning and to develop the concept of 'lifelong learning'.

7 Conclusion: a strategic approach to retail regeneration

The case studies demonstrate numerous useful approaches to retail revitalisation which can inspire innovation elsewhere. The many different approaches confirm that there is no set pattern of appropriate responses to retail decline. The best approaches are fashioned locally, to account for market variations and local factors, but also to ensure that local stakeholders have a hand in fashioning solutions of which they take 'ownership', and are therefore committed to their achievement.

There is growing discussion about the need for retail strategies. This applies not only to shopping centres in designated regeneration areas, which may be badly off but also have significant financial and organisational resources available to them, but also to many declining neighbourhood and district high streets. Unfortunately, trends to larger-format stores, which sell food, electrical goods, clothes, shoes, toys and other products, and include a chemist, newsagent, off-licence, baker, fishmonger and other in-store shops, suggest that many districts and neighbourhoods may continue to face contraction and decline. This may be offset by the advent of small-format chain stores, but not to the extent that the decline is reversed. The issue is whether decline is managed, proactively, to stave off its worst effects and secure the benefits of retail expansion and efficiency without condemning local areas to dereliction. Case studies like Hulme, Castlemilk, Crown Street, Castle Vale and others suggest that new developments that also secure local benefits are far superior to simply letting the market dictate events.

The PAT 13 Report suggested that local forums be established to develop retail strategies. Similarly, a response by many local authorities to out-of-town shopping has been introduction of town centre management (TCM) partnerships. Most regeneration areas already have numerous partnerships in place. However, it is also the case that many stakeholders are suffering from 'partnership fatigue'. Recommendations for additional partnerships should recognise this. This chapter suggests the emerging mechanism of Community Planning should be the means to achieve retail strategies and streamlined partnerships, which are not 'talking shops'.

The dynamic nature of retailing also requires business strategies. The experience of Tesco and Sainsbury's reported here, and retailers like Boots in playing an active role in TCM, suggest that business strategies can be extended to encompass social and environmental objectives, and that there is much potential in a partnership approach which includes retailers and traders' associations. However, many retailers and traders see little benefit in partnership activity, and might need positive encouragement to recognise that they have an important contribution to make to a healthy retail and social environment.

Following from the case studies, this chapter confirms that a strategic, participative approach to retail revival is the best way to foster the kind of innovation reported here, and to help retail partnerships overcome the constraints identified. The term 'strategic' refers to a longer-term perspective that realises economic, social and environmental benefits simultaneously. This is accomplished by vertical integration between a national policy framework conducive to retail revival, appropriate regional planning guidance and the development of local retail strategies, at local authority and district/neighbourhood levels. The term 'participative' refers to the mechanism of partnership, which here is defined in the context of Community Planning.

Retail strategy in planning

PPG 6 sets out the Government's objectives, including focusing retail development in locations where the proximity of businesses facilitates competition from which consumers benefit and which maximise opportunities for transport other than the car (DETR, 1996). The guidance states that it is not the role of the planning system to restrict competition, preserve existing commercial interests or prevent innovation. There is also acceptance that attempts to promote past pattern of uses against market trends that led to the original deterioration are unlikely to be successful. However, this may not be sufficient in that it fails to recognise:

- the significant role that planning policy and transport investments have played in decline of traditional retail patterns

- the social significance that many residents attach to neighbourhood centres, even if they also shop elsewhere to save money, and their importance to non-car and vulnerable households

- the potential of revitalised local shopping areas to contribute to reductions in transport emissions by fostering sustainable transport modes.

Retail policy is set out in development plans and these generally contain policies to enhance and promote the town centre and set out a retail hierarchy which forms the basis of the sequential test used to assess new development. Policy is well meaning in its support for town centre function, but not yet sophisticated enough to take into account the need for town centre vitality *and* area regeneration.

There is no explicit advice within the guidance on the need or content of retail strategies at the development plan (local authority) or district/neighbourhood level. Nor is there any obligation to secure social as well as economic benefits from the location of retail investment, beyond vague discussion of 'providing for people's day-to-day needs'. Given the volume of retail investment in Britain, and the potential contribution to regeneration indicated in the case studies, an approach more fine-tuned to social needs is indicated. Providing it is applied fairly to all retailers, and that retail location is supported by other planning and transport decisions, no disadvantage ought to occur.

Local authorities also face difficulty over whether to allow new development where retailers are most keen, that is near car-owning prosperous households, or to attempt to steer it towards deprived neighbourhoods. However, where town centres are functioning well and there is less available property, development can be steered to regeneration areas and this is a positive outcome of the current policy approach that needs only to be reinforced. Again, there is not a right answer, but the best answers will be derived in discussion, which local authorities enter armed with a high degree of intelligence about trends in the retail sector and how they relate to regeneration, social inclusion, sustainable development and other matters for which they uphold the public, long-term interest.

Local authorities are also concerned that developments that they do not accept wholeheartedly will simply go over to the next authority. This can have a detrimental impact on their willingness to steer retailing towards more marginal and peripheral areas. In large urban areas, a wider strategic approach to the planning of new retail developments is required to prevent the 'ambitions' of individual authorities from having a negative impact on deprived neighbourhoods. Issues concerning the beneficial location of retail investment between competing local authorities need to be resolved within regional planning guidance that recognises the influence it will have on the outcome of regeneration programmes. For too long, land use planning and regeneration have been seen as unrelated fields of policy. A more joined-up approach is suggested.

Recommendation to embed sustainability criteria in regeneration strategy

With a few exceptions, there is little evidence of sustainability criteria, such as for reduced vehicle emissions, having impact in the case studies or in overall regeneration strategy. Yet, nowhere is the need more vital than in regeneration areas where environmental quality impacts on economic and social development, such as retention of inward investment and attraction of new residents to stem population outflow. It also impacts quality of life of socially excluded households, who are more dependent on 'public goods' than well-off households who use private buying power to offset low quality

in public provision. Strategies too often are dominated by an attitude that, given the economic decline suffered by such areas, almost any form of inward investment is better than none with sustainability a luxury for a future time. Yet, these areas offer a real opportunity to create a 'win–win' situation of sustainability *and* social inclusion, and to shift the urban agenda in a sustainable direction with models of good practice. With a few inspiring exceptions, such as at Crown Street or Hulme, this nettle is not being grasped. Sustainability only comes about from linking national and regional policy to local action.

Recommendation on national planning guidance

National planning guidance should be enhanced to foster strategic retail planning at the regional and development plan spatial levels. It should also identify key factors of analysis which enable retail trends, transport and land use planning options and the need to balance town centre and district and neighbourhood function at a time of contracting opportunity for smaller, independent retailers. An appropriate balance of retail function in prosperous and deprived areas should also receive attention, by making the sequential test yet more sophisticated. National planning guidance should more overtly address sustainability issues, such as the need to reduce CO_2 emissions.

Recommendation on revision of PPG 6 to further encompass social and environmental factors

PPG 6 should give greater emphasis to the social and environmental impact of the location of new retail development, particularly superstores and supermarkets. Preference should be given to sites that not only serve areas that have no existing stores but also whose residents have limited access to alternatives. Car ownership, income levels and economic activity indicators could assess this. These criteria should be included in the sequential test. Conversely, supermarket and other retail developments should not be permitted in areas where they would have a detrimental impact on the success of any area regeneration programme, and thus contribute to social exclusion.

Recommendation on regional planning guidance

Regional planning guidance (for England, and its equivalent for Wales and Scotland) should integrate need for retail vitality and area regeneration within the broader context of integration of transport and land use. The need to reduce CO_2 emissions by planning should also feature strongly in guidance. Parking charges at most retail locations, in and out of town, should be considered, including the opportunity to hypothecate parking revenues to sustainable transport modes.

Recommendation on local authority development plans

The 'hierarchical' framework for retailing which enables sequential testing should be developed, to encompass the need for support for regeneration, and district and neighbourhood centres. Local authorities' development plans should encompass retail analysis and 25 strategies for retail location and enhancement.

Retail strategies at neighbourhood and district level

Within the context of the development plan, regeneration areas and any other neighbourhood concerned about the quality and future of its shopping area would be wise to organise itself to develop partnership and strategy. At the very least, the partnership unlocks information and good ideas about how to tackle existing problems, and the strategy can be used as a bargaining point in discussion with local authorities and other stakeholders. A successful retail strategy will have to take into account the viability of retail businesses, the requirements of planning policy and guidance, and the aspirations of the local residents. Every local retail strategy includes the following objectives:

- increase existing retail provision
- strengthen the provision of associated services
- improve the shopping environment
- promote and market the shopping centre.

Recommendation for neighbourhood/district retail strategies

The decline of local retail viability and vitality should be managed and countered within the context of both top-down development planning and local, bottom-up retail development strategies, which encompass residents' social and environmental aspirations. Retail development partnerships (or forums) need to engage in a tangible process of strategy development to be productive and meaningful for participants and to achieve positive outcomes.

These key points have been developed into an outline blueprint for a local strategy approach, summarised in Appendix 1. Implementation of local retail strategies will benefit from assistance from a local council officer with specialised retail expertise, and in the context of emerging Community Planning initiatives.

Recommendation for local authority liaison officer on retail enhancement

Every local authority concerned about the quality of retailing in and out of regeneration areas would benefit from designating an officer to develop intelligence and competence in this area. The officer would be available to assist local retail development partnerships with retail assessment and strategy, to monitor retail viability and vitality, and to promote the case for retail area enhancement within planning and economic development processes. They could liaise with other stakeholders over key issues of concern such as bus transport or public safety.

Recommendation for local retail development initiatives within the context of the Community Planning framework

PAT 13's call for local retail forums is a reasonable start, but there is a danger these will be discredited as 'talking shops' unless they are focused on strategy in a context that allows tangible achievement. This context means they do not duplicate existing partnership efforts, that they are in a position to drive forward a retail regeneration strategy that has a reasonable chance of success, and that non-council stakeholders have a straightforward means to interact with the local council. The emerging Community Planning framework, at the neighbourhood or area level, provides the best context for this.

For a local authority, this may mean dealing simultaneously with numerous retail development initiatives. Most regeneration areas have existing partnerships and Local Strategic Partnerships (LSPs) are emerging to co-ordinate regeneration activities. There have already been many calls for integration of LSPs into Community Planning. Overall, each neighbourhood would benefit from a single development strategy and a single organisational framework for taking this forward.

Notes

Chapter 1

1 Vitality is a measure of how busy a retail area is, often measured in terms of 'footfall' of passing customers. Viability is a measure of a retail area's capacity to attract ongoing investment for maintenance, improvement and adaptation to remain competitive (NPPG 8).

Chapter 2

1 And a 'basket' of six other greenhouse gases by 12.5 per cent.

2 A sequential approach means that first preference in the siting of any retail development should be for town centre sites, where suitable sites or buildings appropriate for conversion are available, followed by edge-of-centre sites, district and local centres and only then out-of-centre sites in locations that are accessible by a choice of means of transport, rather than the car alone. (PPG 6 para. 1.11).

Chapter 3

1 As to the mechanism of setting rates, all non-domestic property is revalued every five years by an independent valuation officer of the Valuation Office Agency. The last revaluation was 1 April 2000 and the rateable value of property represents its annual open market rental value as at 1 April 1998. The valuation officer may alter the value if he believes that the circumstances of the property have changed, or the ratepayer may propose a change in value. If ratepayer and valuation officer do not agree, the matter is referred on appeal to a valuation tribunal. A national non-domestic rating multiplier is then used to calculate the annual rate bill for a property. It is set annually by the Government and, except in a revaluation year, cannot by law rise more than the amount of increase in the retail price index. Therefore, very roughly, a business will be paying approximately half as much in business rate as it does in rent.

Chapter 4

1 Arts Factory has 1,300 members, 25 staff and over 100 volunteers. It owns and manages community businesses, including in the areas of environmental art, graphic design, video production, woodworking and a garden centre. Its range of operation, and fusing of commercial income with subsidy to fight social exclusion, is typical of many CDTs.

References

Acheson, Sir. D. (1998) *Independent Inquiry into Inequalities in Health Report*. London: The Stationery Office

Bonnel, P. (1995) 'Urban car policy in Europe', *Transport Policy*, Vol. 2, No. 2, pp. 83–95

Boots the Chemists (1998) *Impact of Out-of-centre Food Superstores on Local Retail Employment*. Nottingham: Boots the Chemists/National Retail Planning Forum

Boots the Chemists and Civic Trust (1996) *Caring for Our Towns and Cities*. Nottingham: Boots the Chemists

Cameron, C. (2000) Chair, UK LA21 Steering Group, speaking at Leadership for Well-being Conference, Royal Society for the Arts

Carley, M. (1992) 'Settlement trends and the crisis of automobility', *Futures*, Vol. 24, pp. 206–18

Carley, M. (1996) *Sustainable Transport and Retail Vitality: State of the Art for Towns and Cities*. Edinburgh: Scottish Historic Burghs Association and Donaldsons, Chartered Surveyors

Carley, M. (1999) 'Neighbourhoods – building blocks of national sustainable development', *Town and Country Planning*, February, pp. 58–61

Carley, M. and Christie, I. (2000) *Managing Sustainable Development*. Revised edition. London: Kogan Page Earthscan

Carley, M. and Spapins, P. (1998) *Sharing the World: Sustainable Living and Global Equity in the 21st Century*. London: Kogan Page Earthscan

Carley, M. et al. (2000a) *Urban Regeneration through Partnership: A Study in Nine Urban Regions in England, Scotland and Wales*. Bristol: The Policy Press

Carley, M. et al. (2000b) *Area Regeneration in the 21st Century*. Bristol: The Policy Press

Castlemilk Umbrella Group (1989) 'A tale of two Castlemilks: the community response', unpublished report

Chase, M., Burnett, J. and Buchanan, M. (1997) *The Health of Historic Towns in Scotland*. Edinburgh: Historic Burghs Association Research Paper

Colliers Erdman Lewis (1999) *Midsummer Retail Report*. London: Colliers Erdman Lewis

Department of the Environment, Transport and the Regions (DETR) (1996) *Revised PPG6 Town Centres and Retail Developments*. London: HMSO

Department of the Environment, Transport and the Regions (DETR) (2000) *Preparing Community Strategies: Draft Guidance to Local Authorities*. London: DETR

Ecotec Research and Consulting and Transportation Planning Consultants (1993) *Reducing Transport Emissions through Planning*. London: HMSO

EDAW for Tesco (1999) The impact of out-of-town food superstores on local retail employment: a critique of Boots/NRPF research', unpublished report

Glass, A. and McGregor, A. (2000) *Braehead Recruitment and Training Initiative and Evaluation – Final Report*. Glasgow: Training and Employment Research Unit, University of Glasgow

Hillier Parker (1997) *The Impact of Large Foodstores on Market Towns and District Centres*. London

Houghton, J. (1997) *Global Warming: The Complete Briefing*. Cambridge: Cambridge University Press

House of Commons Environment Committee (1994) *Shopping Centres and their Future*. 4th Report. London: House of Commons Environment Committee

Hulme Regeneration Ltd (1994) *Hulme – a Guide to Development*. Manchester: Hulme Regeneration Ltd

Institute for Fiscal Studies (1995) *The Relationship between Rates and Rents*. London: Local Government Research Unit DETR

London Economics (1995) *The Economics of Employment in Grocery Retailing*. London: London Economics

Monopolies Commission (2000) *A Summary of Supermarkets: A Report on the Supply of Groceries from Multiple Stores in the United Kingdom*. London: Monopolies Commission

National Retail Planning Forum Research Group (1997) *Out-of-town Supermarkets and Local Retail Employment*. London: National Retail Planning Forum

Robinson, N., Caraher, M. and Lang, T. (2000) 'Access to shops: the views of low-income shoppers', *Health Education Journal*, Vol. 59, pp. 121–36

Select Committee on Environment, Transport and Regional Affairs (1999) Second Report *Environmental Impact of Supermarket Competition*. London: Select Committee on Environment, Transport and Regional Affairs

(The) Independent (1998a) 'Tesco to serve up new jobs for 10,000', 23 September

(The) Independent (1998b) 'Historic town set for battle with Tesco', 17 December

(The) Independent (1999a) 'Boots to expand out-of-town', 9 September

(The) Independent (1999b) 'Wal-Mart roll-back hits high street', 14 October

(The) Observer (1999) 'The store that ate America', 26 September

Townsend, A., Sadler, D. and Hudson, R. (1996) 'Geographical dimensions of UK retailing employment change', in N. Wrigley and M. Lowe *Retailing, Consumption and Capital: Towards a New Retail Geography*. Harlow: Longman

URBED (1994) *Vital and Viable Town Centres: Meeting the Challenge*. London: Department of the Environment

Appendix 1

Blueprint for a local retail analysis

1 Undertake SWOT analysis of existing facilities

This should include a land-use survey plotting all the retail facilities in the area. The following should be included:

- type of shop
- floor space, to calculate potential demand
- vacant units
- condition of building and surrounding environment
- rental levels.

The information forms the baseline for the strategy. A decision needs to be made regarding the boundaries of the study because there may be shops outside the study, in neighbouring areas, whose catchment area extends into the study area.

2 Consult owners of retail property

This not only allows their future plans to be determined, it also encourages their involvement in the regeneration of the area. There may be potential difficulties if the retailers feel threatened by new proposals, particularly if they have a monopoly in the area. Shopping centres may be owned by one company or organisation, which may have different views from the individual shopkeepers.

3 Survey residents and local shops over key issues; analyse gaps in provision and potential for development

To identify and understand existing shopping habits, to find out why or why not residents use the existing shops and where they do, their habits and patterns of expenditure. The survey also helps determine what demand there is for different facilities within the area including services such as health facilities, hairdressers, banks and local council offices. The case studies demonstrate introduction of these uses can all help improve footfall and therefore vitality and viability. The local retailers will be able to advise on shopping patterns in their own outlets. The residents' and shop survey should also identify other issues such as transport quality, environment, crime and public safety concerns. This will form the basis of the retail strategy but, in order for it to be implemented, it needs the support of the community, local authority and retailers.

4 Organise relevant stakeholders

Consultation and surveys put the organising team in touch with many stakeholders; others, such as the Employment Service or the police may need to be contacted. An appropriate partnership needs to be developed, within the existing context of partnership or from scratch but mindful of the need to avoid duplication of effort. There is much guidance on the development of partnership and participation (Carley *et al.*, 2000b).

5 Identify suitable locations and sites for new development

A decision may have to be made on whether to retain existing shops, particularly if they are in a poor condition and suffer from a bad reputation, maybe as a result of crime and anti-social behaviour. A balance also has to be made between locations that offer commercial viability and the potential catchment area of customers. These sites need to be pursued through the wider regeneration strategy and local plan.

6 Promote local or district centre as a location for new retail development

This promotion has to go further than including the sites in the local plan. The sites need to be actively marketed by the local authority and owners. This marketing should be supported by the data from the residents' survey to demonstrate potential demand. Owners should be encouraged to provide incentives to encourage new businesses and employment training.

7 Identify critical elements of the shopping centre

While planning policy cannot protect individual shopping units and prevent competition, it can be used to protect viability of existing centres. It is therefore important to identify particular services or shops that are critical to the viability of the centre and seek to protect them in planning policy and planning conditions on new development. For example, conditions can prevent supermarkets from opening pharmacies or post offices.

8 Improve public transport access, walking and cycling provision, and car parking facilities

Public transport within the regeneration area may be limited and/or the pricing structure may encourage residents to use other larger shopping centres because it is no more expensive to travel there. Bus companies need to be brought into discussions early to ensure services and routes at the appropriate time. The bus station outside the Tesco in Seacroft is a good example.

Access for walk-in and cycling customers should be reviewed to encourage more visitors using sustainable transport modes. Improvements are frequently linked with increased security to reduce the fear of crime. A feature of declining shopping centres is ample car parking of poor quality and perceived to be insecure. The ability to attract customers from outside the area has wider benefits than just making the shopping centre more viable; it can also help to reduce the stigma of the area. Any increase in traffic levels should be carefully managed.

In certain neighbourhoods, it may be concluded that access to improved shopping facilities can be met by improving, and increasing access to, existing retail facilities. This could be assisted by encouraging the retailers to provide free transport and/or delivery services.

9 Consider high street or shopping centre manager

Potential for appointment of a centre manager to promote the shopping and to co-ordinate marketing, security and environmental improvement – some neighbourhood retail areas may be too small to justify a full-time appointment but there can be scope to link up a number of similar neighbourhoods under one manager.

10 Target new facilities at potential new residents and customers; increase catchment where feasible

While it is important to provide improved facilities for the existing residents, the case studies demonstrate that success of a shopping centre will also be dependent on attracting new customers, or even new residents through housing initiatives, as in Crown Street. Retail strategy needs to be linked to the overall regeneration.

11 Consider innovative means of marketing and promotion

The case studies, particularly for Green Street and Borough Market, suggested many innovative means for promotion including use of newspapers, magazines, radio, television, poster and bus advertising, and local promotions in association with traders. Professional advice should be secured where possible.

Appendix 2
Retail food formats – a guide

The major supermarket chains have each developed common formats and designs for their stores, which are heavily branded. Prior to 1980, this was based on similar-sized stores of around 3,000 sq. m. In the 1980s, relaxation of planning policy, the availability of greenfield sites and increased demand for economies of scale drove up the size of stores and increased the range of goods sold to include clothes and household goods. The re-emergence of stronger planning controls in the 1990s has limited the availability of sites and caused the major retailers to widen their range of outlets. For example, Tesco now has five basic store types (see Table A2.1) with other retailers mirroring some or all of this range of formats, but with Asda Wal-Mart now proposing stores of 180,000 sq. ft.

The past two decades have also seen discount traders moving into the market, such as the UK-based Kwik Save and the European traders Aldi, Netto and Lidl – all of which are frequently found in regeneration areas. Such discount supermarkets are able to offer lower prices because they offer a smaller range of goods, sometimes of unfamiliar brands, and more cost-effective (i.e. cheaper) displays and store environment. There is also the emergence of the 'warehouse club' format, involving nominal membership and trading from huge, inexpensive sheds, such as Costco.

Table A2.1 The five basic types of Tesco store

Type	Description
Extra or Hypermarket	Major sub-regional destination store of up to 110,000 sq. ft, in which grocery shopping is supplemented by electrical goods, clothing, a chemist, toys and other products.
Superstore	The traditional out-of-town supermarket of 40,000 to 70,000 sq. ft, offering a wide range of goods with car parking and a full range of services.
Compact	This is a smaller store but still offering a wider range of goods. It is more likely to be located within a built-up area but still with car parking available.
Metro	Frequently located in the traditional high street or city centre and offering a limited range of goods with emphasis on convenience foods. Represents a return to town centre locations, but with a product range oriented to the shopper in nearby employment. Car parking not necessary. Sometimes called 'Local'.
Express	Combines a petrol forecourt and convenience store offering goods similar to a neighbourhood or village grocery shop.